CAN
GOD
BE
TRUSTED?

CAN GOD BE TRUSTED?

Finding Faith in Troubled Times

Thomas D. Williams, LC, ThD

New York Boston Nashville

CONTENTS

INTRODUCTION

This book came about in a funny way. When I was in New York presenting an earlier book on the spiritual life, *Spiritual Progress*, someone asked me a question that threw me for a minor loop. Rather than ask for an explanation of *Spiritual Progress*, one man asked whether there was anything I had *wanted* to write about but didn't. I paused for a moment, somewhat taken aback by the question. But then the answer came to me quickly: "Trust in God." I had even included a chapter on trust in God in my original outline, but I had run out of both space and time. "I guess that will be your next book," the man replied. That night, our little exchange played over and over again in my mind as I lay awake in bed.

Back in Rome, I started bouncing the idea off friends and colleagues. I even came up with what I thought was a clever working title—*Can God Be Trusted?*—playing off the slogan on U.S. currency. Yet I never expected the reaction I got. I was with a friend named Jeff one evening, and I told him of the project, nonchalantly throwing out my title idea. Jeff suddenly got serious, looked me right in the eye, and asked: "Well, can he?"

"Can he what?" I answered, honestly confused by the question.

"Can he be trusted? Can God be trusted? What's the answer to your question?"

Up till that moment I really hadn't thought of the title as anything more than a catchy, rhetorical question. I assumed that the answer was obvious. Over the following months I realized it wasn't obvious at all.

Granted, in my years as a spiritual counselor I had often encountered people with trust issues. It seems that everyone, in fact, has trouble trusting God at some point in his or her life. Our modern trust issues aren't limited to God either. It is rightly said that our civilization is undergoing a profound crisis of trust. Think of emotional relationships, for instance. Look at the way people put off marriage, afraid of both others' infidelity and their own! Others sign prenuptial agreements covering everything from the division of assets to how many times a month they can expect to have intercourse. In business relationships, too, a simple handshake no longer means anything. We need to bring in a lawyer to draft a detailed contract outlining every aspect of our arrangement so we will have legal recourse "if need be." Having been let down so many times, we no longer trust our government, our spouses, our friends, or even our parents and siblings.

But this trust crisis does extend to God as well. In my experience, in fact, there seems to be nothing more difficult than maintaining a real, unshakable trust in God throughout life. The problem of rampant evil in the world, natural disasters, and the suffering of children and innocent people all throw our naive confidence off balance. But it is when we experience a personal letdown that we truly begin to doubt. Personal tragedy, unfulfilled aspirations, and the "silence" of God in our lives can all lead to profound desperation. Some become "realists," and others sink into cynicism and nihilism.

But it is one thing to have trouble trusting—no matter how difficult—and another thing altogether to question God's trustworthiness. For some reason I assumed that people generally believed God was trustworthy. Jeff's question caused me to seriously doubt that assumption.

Realizing my fundamental error, I decided that *Can God Be Trusted?* would be different from previous books. I wouldn't just tell readers what I thought about trust in God, or even what the Bible teaches. I decided to try to find out what other people think about trusting God and the real hurdles they face in doing so. I assembled a small team of researchers, and together we interviewed hundreds of people on the issue of trust in God: young, old, male, female, believers, and nonbelievers alike. The results were both surprising and enriching. I will share some of those results with you throughout this book, interspersing real-life testimonies with my own reflections and questions. I hope the results please you as much as they have pleased me.

I will, however, tip my hand regarding *my* answer to this question. I am not an unbiased observer with no opinion on the matter. You probably won't be surprised to learn that I believe God is totally and absolutely trustworthy. I believe, in fact, that in a world that often seems to be made of quicksand, God is the only truly rock-solid ground that exists. And I bet that wherever you stand and whatever personal experiences you have had, you *want* that to be true. You would like me to convince you that you can trust God. We would all like to believe that the world makes sense, and part of that sense means there is a good and loving God who can make everything all right. But we don't want anyone to pull the wool over our eyes either. If God cannot be trusted, we want to know it once and for all. There's no sense in believing in fairy tales.

Part of this exploration will involve trying to understand what we can expect from God and what we shouldn't expect from him. Surely some of our disappointments with God stem from expecting the wrong things, things he never promised or intended to give.

It seems to me that in the midst of all our reasons not to trust, God continues to invite us to confidence in him. He looks us in the eye and asks us, even begs us, to believe. He insists that he loves us, he has a plan, and in the end everything will work out if we stick with him.

So, along with the real, personal experiences and moving testimonies I will share with you, I will also make a case for trust in God. I will give you what I believe to be some solid reasons to lean on him, to rely on him, and for some of you, to give him a second chance. Maybe someday you can share your story with me.

WHY
TRUST
MATTERS

I

THE DOWNSIDE OF DISTRUST

Blessed are the pessimists—it is sometimes said—for they will never be disappointed. There is some truth to that. The one who expects nothing can never be let down. Hope and trust are scary things. We risk betrayal and disappointment. We risk abandonment and disillusion. It is much safer to hope for nothing, desire nothing, aspire to nothing.

In our crazy, mixed-up world, distrust has become something of an ideal. We don't want to be anybody's fool. We would do anything to avoid being taken advantage of like some naive simpleton, duped by the first shyster to come along. So we protect and defend ourselves against any sort of con. We make distrust a *virtue*.

A story is told of a New York lawyer who one day calls his ten-year-old son in for a lesson. He has the child stand on a chair with his back to his father, then tells him to close his eyes and fall backward, promising to catch him. The young son is hesitant at first, but since it's his father, he eventually does as he is told. As soon as he closes his eyes and plunges backward his father steps out of the way, allowing his son to come crashing to the ground. Bruised and crying, the son struggles to his feet, glaring at his father and asking, "But why? Why?" The father replies, "Sorry, son, but the most important lesson you have to learn in this life is that you can't trust anyone, not even your father."

For most of us, this story is heart-wrenching. Who is capable of such cynicism, robbing a boy of his innocence at such an early age? Yet when you think about it, this is a key message of today's society. Better to distrust a thousand times when you could have trusted than to trust even once and be betrayed. There are few things we disdain more than gullibility.

Our hostility toward naïveté goes hand in hand with our love of self-sufficiency. It is truly the American ideal. We are raised with a default mentality of self-help and self-reliance. We learn to do things ourselves, to think for ourselves, and to solve our own problems. We are critical and questioning, responsible and autonomous. We are self-made and self-sustaining.

Think of how important it is in our society to show that we didn't get a free ride. How many fathers and mothers talk about how tough they had it when they were children? People speak with evident pride about how they held down three jobs to pay their way through college, or how they worked their way up from janitor to become CEO of the company. These rags-to-riches stories of personal achievement fill us with admiration and make us want to be like these self-made heroes.

I'm a scientist so I'm really not into anything like that [trust in God]. I believe in evolution and God had nothing to do with it.

—JAMES, AGE 34

Our movies, too, teem with models of this sort: the maverick who takes on the system, the lone vigilante who brings criminals to justice, the stop-at-nothing journalist who digs and digs till she unearths the true story. We revel in these accounts of individuals who did it all on their own, despite the resistance of others. Their suspicion of others was vindicated, their distrust justified. *Trust no one but yourself.*

SPIRITUAL AUTONOMY

We can carry this mentality over into even our spiritual lives. Talk of a Savior and forgiveness and God's grace makes us uncomfortable. That is for the weak. Trust in God is for those who have run out of other options and are brought to their knees by circumstances outside their control. We prefer to be self-justifying. We want to be our own saviors. Just tell us the rules, and we will achieve greatness—not a shared greatness where God steals our thunder, but personal, individual greatness with no one to thank but ourselves.

What is self-righteousness, after all, if not the conviction that we have no need of assistance—human or divine—to reach moral purity? The self-righteous are proud in their subjective assurance that they have never needed God's mercy. They know—in theory—that God is merciful, but they believe this is a chip they have never needed to cash in, like a trapeze artist who has never needed the escape net that waits below. They know that if—God forbid!—they ever really needed his mercy (in a serious way, and not for their little peccadilloes), they could get down on their knees and ask for it. Yet—thank God!—that has never been the case. They believe that they have taken the high road of righteousness, over the low road—the cop-out—of those who have needed to appeal to God's mercy and grace. They aren't saddened at never having experienced God's forgiveness; they are proud of it. Mercy is for the weak folk, the economy-class Christians, the "sinners."

These self-made Christians are the sort who see another person doing something wrong and smile smugly, announcing with evident relish that so-and-so will get his comeuppance on Judgment Day! Rather than longing for sinners' conversion and salvation, they yearn for divine retribution. *People must answer for their actions. Each person makes his or her bed and must lie in it.* Their God is a God of justice, rubbing his hands in anxious anticipation of punishing recalcitrant sinners. Mercy is an unfortunate addendum to the gospel, a concession made in order not to frighten people away from the overarching truth that God is *just.* No favors. No plea bargaining. No quarter requested, and none given.

Few would articulate their beliefs in these terms, but many live this way. Last year I met a young man named Nicola who summed up his beliefs like this: "I believe God gives us one chance, but not two. If we blow it, that's it. It's our choice. And that's the way we should be with other people. Give them one opportunity to prove themselves. But after that, there's no coming back and begging for a second chance."

This spiritual model is a natural offshoot from the self-sufficiency I described a moment ago. Radical independence leaves no room for reliance on anyone, not even God. Distrust of others and self-reliance go together like eggs and bacon.

CRACKS IN THE THEORY

Yet I would like to venture an unpopular thesis. Self-sufficiency is a destructive myth and a bad model. It is destructive first because it is a lie. After all, as much as we would like to think we've always done everything on our own, we haven't. We didn't create ourselves, give birth to ourselves, feed ourselves when small, educate ourselves, or take care of ourselves when we were sick. We benefit from books others wrote, eat food that others grew, make use of technology that others developed, and enjoy a freedom that others fought and died for.

But even beyond our objective dependence on others, self-sufficiency is a bad model and a false ideal. It is *unworthy* of pursuit. Even if we could reach a state of absolute self-reliance, in so doing we would have ruined and dehumanized ourselves. In distrusting others we may think we're smarter than the rest, but in the end we become profoundly unhappy. We work and work at reaching self-sufficiency, and just when we get there we realize it leaves us empty. We cut our reliance on others to the point that we become islands, neither trusting others nor allowing others to depend on us, only to find that an island is an unhappy soul.

Think of the real-life people you know who most closely resemble the "self-made man" I have just described. Think of a person you know who depends on no one, trusts no one, and attempts to do everything for himself or herself. Someone like Howard Hughes or Citizen Kane. Now ask yourself: *Is this person happy? Has this person reached the ideal that we should all aspire to? In becoming self-sufficient, what has this person had to sacrifice? Was it worth it?* Many times, in seeming to achieve everything, such a person really loses everything that really matters. "What does it profit them if they gain the whole world, but lose or forfeit themselves?" (Luke 9:25).

Granted, responsibility, know-how, and critical thinking are all noble and worthy goals. We should aspire to a certain degree of self-reliance, but not to the exclusion of trust and interdependence. Responsibility is praiseworthy until it reaches the point that we rely *only* on ourselves. By assuming the worst of others, we belittle ourselves and hole ourselves up behind a wall of our own making. In its worst expressions, habitual distrust leads to fear and paranoia (think again of Howard Hughes); but even in its more mitigated forms, it detracts from the person and undermines relationships.

How did this situation come about? How did we reach the point that distrust is no longer a vice to overcome, but rather a virtue to pursue? There are undoubtedly many historical and cultural reasons, along with the recent breakdown of family life and the pandemic of broken promises. But I would like to point to another cause, more subtle but even more decisive.

THE ORIGINAL DECEIT

To ask where distrust comes from, we must ask where human sin came from, because sin and distrust are strangely related. What first brought it about? The Bible tells a story of the fall of man, the first sin of human beings. No matter what you may think about the historical accuracy of every detail chronicled in the first chapters of the book of Genesis, the narration is worth contemplating. It reveals deep truths about the human condition and our broken relationship with our Creator.

What we most often fail to realize is that original *sin* is fruit of the original *lie*. The devil doesn't start off by simply inviting Eve to sin. He starts by questioning her and getting her to question God. He asks with mock innocence: "Did God say, 'You shall not eat from any tree in the garden'?" (Gen. 3:1). The devil knows full well what God had commanded, but he wants Eve to start analyzing God's command and to question its reasonableness. Then he can provide an alternative account, contradicting God's version: "But the serpent said to the woman, 'You will not die; for God knows that when you eat of it your eyes will be opened, and you will be like God, knowing good and evil'" (Gen. 3:4–5). The devil's lie can be summarized: *God is not to be trusted*. Before Satan induced Eve to sin, he had to undermine her trust in God. He had to sow suspicion regarding God's motives. Only when Eve began to doubt God's goodness was she ready to disobey him. And once Eve doubted God, the Fall was inevitable.[1]

The scary thing is this: the devil's MO hasn't changed. He still seeks to sow distrust. More than anything else, the devil wishes to separate us from God, and the only way to do that is by undercutting our trust in him. The less we trust in God, the more alone we feel in the universe. Instead of getting "smarter," we simply become disconnected.

> *I don't believe God should be trusted. God doesn't need to be trusted. We have our own decisions to make and that's all there is to it. God can do as he pleases.*
>
> —SIMON, AGE 28

DISTRUST DESTROYS THE SOCIAL FABRIC

The devil's lie didn't only break down our trust in him; it also destroyed our trust in one another. Genuine community is based on trust. Without trust, no society can stand for long. Look what happened in countries behind the Iron Curtain during the long reign of Communism. I spoke with a man who lived in the Soviet Union all his life. He told me that living in Communist Russia, you never knew who the spies were. People informed on their neighbors, their parents, their children, their colleagues, and their teachers. Everyone you met was a possible government informant. People lived in terror, never knowing whom they could trust. At that time, you learned never to share your thoughts with anyone else and to live behind locked doors.

The man who explained all this to me told me that even now, years later, he finds it hard to trust. He finds it hard to look people in the eye, for fear they should see something and report it. Fear and distrust go together. To live in distrust is to live in fear. We dare not trust, because we are afraid of what could happen if the other person betrayed us.

We shouldn't think that this sad scenario is just the stuff of totalitarian states. Our democratic society also depends on trust and breaks down when distrust takes over. To take one mundane example, look at how companies vie for the public's trust. They bend over backward to gain consumer confidence and hold it. This is essential for their image and profits. There is no better long-term guarantee of sales than customer loyalty, based on trust in a company and its products.

A simple survey of ad slogans for major products and services reveals an astonishing recurrence to the trust motif. In its publicity the abortion provider Planned Parenthood claims to offer "info you can trust" on sexuality and relationships. The Everpure Company sells "water you can trust." SolidSkate manufactures "longboard skateboards you can trust." The firm Kan Herb offers "Chinese herbal products you can trust." Cyberauthorize doesn't beat around the bush but claims to be simply "the company you can trust." In fact, nowadays it's almost impossible to find a company that doesn't proclaim its trustworthiness as a key reason for buying its products or using its services.

For this reason, companies invest huge sums of research and advertising money to prove that their products and services are reliable. As a kid, I was accustomed to hearing television ads for Trident gum that authoritatively announced, "Four out of five dentists surveyed recommend sugarless gum for their patients who chew gum." I must say that this slogan had a real effect on me. For years I have chewed nothing but sugarless gum. Now I don't know whether the claim is actually true. How many dentists were surveyed, for instance, to obtain the figure of "four out of five"? I certainly never actually asked a dentist whether he recommended chewing sugarless gum (though I have no doubt that he *would*). The point is that the slogan won me over, and I've been chewing sugarless gum ever since.

But the contrary is also true. There is nothing like consumer *distrust* to crush a company's success. Do you remember the Tylenol scare in the autumn of 1982? Seven people in the Chicago area died after ingesting Extra

Strength Tylenol capsules laced with potassium cyanide. In the aftermath of the incident, Johnson & Johnson, Tylenol's parent company, halted Tylenol production and advertising. A nationwide recall of Tylenol products was issued as well. At the time there were an estimated 31 million bottles in circulation, with a retail value of more than $100 million. As a result, the market share of Tylenol collapsed from 35 percent to 8 percent.[2] After a herculean effort to regain consumer confidence, the company was able to reestablish itself with time, but not all firms are so fortunate.

We can see that distrust not only diminishes us as individuals, it also corrodes our society. Human beings are relational creatures, made to live in community and to work together. The glue that binds us together is a fundamental trust in one another. Distrust dissolves that glue and leaves us alone and isolated. Far from being a virtue, distrust is a cancer that slowly eats away at our personal and social well-being.

Diagnosing the disease is only the first step. We must also find the cure. If distrust is not the way, then what is? What does trust have to offer besides increased exposure and vulnerability? Why is trust a better road? This will be our topic for the next chapter.

2

WHAT MAKES IT ALL WORTHWHILE

Whether we like it or not, we all have to trust others for some things. C. S. Lewis wisely observed that "ninety-nine percent of the things you believe are believed on authority."[1] We have neither the time nor the ability to verify every fact we read in newspapers and history books. We cannot travel to every town and country on the map to personally ascertain their existence. We cannot know everything about medicine to correctly diagnose and resolve our own and our family's health issues, or be experts in plumbing, car repair, investing, jurisprudence, and computer programming and so able to fend for ourselves in each of these areas.

Even scientists, who pride themselves on being skeptical of anything that cannot be empirically demonstrated, live immersed in a world of faith. What chemist has personally verified the atomic weight of every element on the table? What biologist has examined members of every species of plant or animal about which he expounds with absolute certainty and confidence? Much of what scientists take to be true, they take on the word and experience of others. What is true of science is true of every other discipline as well.

History provides a particularly eloquent case in point. In the end, all the historical knowledge in the world is based on authority and trust. No living historian witnessed Hannibal's crossing of the Alps, was present at the Battle of Waterloo, or sat in on the First Continental Congress. The entire science of history is based on trust in the word of others. Trust and dependence on others are, quite simply, necessary for human existence.

Yet trust is risky. Many would never choose to trust, if they had other options. We seek security, and we are right to do so. We like to know that things are in place and taken care of. This is part of what it means to be responsible. We plan ahead and leave as little as possible to chance or fortune. We would naturally prefer to *know* rather than to believe, to *see* rather than to trust, to *possess* now rather than to hope in the future. This is human nature.

So let's imagine for a moment a world where trust wasn't necessary. Let's pretend we could actually eliminate the need for trust, taking care of ourselves in all these dimensions of our lives and experiencing things firsthand without ever having to take another's word for anything. Would the world be a better place? This is an important question for both our human relationships and our relationship with God. Think about this for a moment. As an ideal, should we arrange things to minimize our need to trust others? If it were humanly possible, should we try to eliminate trust altogether from our lives?

If you *could* completely eradicate your need to trust in God or any human person, would you do so? Would this be a victory or a defeat?

That's a tough question. It all boils down to whether we see human trust as a necessary evil or as something good and worthy of pursuit in itself. In many ways, trust seems to be imperfect knowledge and a last resort. We fall back on trust when we are unable to empirically verify things for ourselves. We entrust our needs to others when we are unable to completely take care of them ourselves. We have no other choice.

Yet, in a deeper way, isn't trust somehow part of what makes us truly human? Isn't it an integral part of our friendships, relationships, and spiritual lives, without which our very humanity would dry up and wither away?

MORE TRUSTING, MORE HUMAN

Trust unites people in a way that no other human action can. It isn't the same for two people to work together or play together as it is for them to *trust* each other. There is a bond created from trust that cannot be forged in any other way. In fact, a friendship without trust wouldn't be a real friendship at all, but simply a relationship of utility. Being able to believe in someone means belief in goodness itself.

After being let down a few times, however, we may begin to think this is all a utopia. Sure, we would love to have families where everyone trusted everyone else (and where that trust was always rewarded!). We would love to work in an environment where trust between colleagues reigned, and faithfulness was the order of the day. We would love to live in a society where we didn't have to be careful or suspicious of others, where we could leave our doors unlocked and always assume the best of others' motives. But the sad reality is that this is not what our world is like. We cannot always trust others. We must be careful and prudent. We must protect our vulnerability.

My biggest hurdle in the trust department was the decision to get married. I was engaged to my wife for seven and a half years and kept putting off marriage, to the point that my fiancée was desperate. I loved her and knew she was the one for me, but [I] was so afraid of that commitment. I'm sure it has something to do with my parents' divorce, which left a deep impression on me. Anyway, three years ago we were married. I am so happy and so grateful to God for helping me get over my trust issues.

—JEREMY, AGE 33

In fact, more than a desire for trust, we feel a desire that *others be trustworthy*. We would like them to be faithful to their promises and true to their word. We would like them to be responsible and committed, rather than flighty, self-interested, and sometimes downright thoughtless and cruel. No matter how trusting we are, we won't change other people. So why bother? If my trust cannot make others trustworthy, what is trust worth? In the end, it seems, what we need is more *trustworthiness*, rather than more trust.

I would argue that trust makes us better people. Just as a habitual unwillingness to trust belittles and diminishes us, a willingness to trust makes us bigger and better and makes a true human community possible. This doesn't mean we should trust everyone or expect the same things from every person. Trust is indeed a response to trustworthiness and should not be offered where the latter is not to be found. Yet trustworthiness *does* exist, in varying degrees, all around us. It exists ultimately and perfectly in God. Our openness to trust opens us to the reality of others' goodness.

The 2001 film *A Beautiful Mind* made this point in a lovely way. The movie is based on the true story of John Nash, a brilliant mathematician and Nobel Prize winner. Nash (played by Russell Crowe) suffers from paranoid schizophrenia and experiences delusions, seeing and hearing people who don't really exist. Unable to distinguish between reality and fantasy, Nash finds it nearly impossible to come to grips with his condition. In the end, the only way he can know what is real comes from trusting in his wife, Alicia (Jennifer Connelly). He humbly asks her to help him discern what is real and what is unreal. In this way, love and trust become his only sure link with the real world, his only plank of salvation to which he clings. Despite all his brilliance, it is not his intelligence but trust in another person that makes Nash whole and keeps him in the real world.

Trust is a profoundly human act. It rounds out our humanity and completes us. In his fascinating reflections on the relationship between faith and reason, Pope John Paul II offered an enriching thought regarding the nature of trust. Rather than an imperfect form of knowledge, he argued, trust in others reveals an essential aspect of humanity not found in mere empirical knowledge:

> In believing, we entrust ourselves to the knowledge acquired by other people. This suggests an important tension. On the one hand, the knowledge acquired through belief can seem an imperfect form of knowledge, to be perfected gradually through personal accumulation of evidence; on the other hand, belief is often humanly richer than mere evidence, because it involves an interpersonal relationship and brings into play not only a person's capacity to know but also the

deeper capacity to entrust oneself to others, to enter into a relationship with them which is intimate and enduring.[2]

If this is true, then trust is not merely a stopgap. Not only does it fill in
for us when other, more direct knowledge is unavailable, but it is legitimate
and worthy of pursuit in its own right. Without trust, something is lacking in our lives. *Even so*—you may be thinking—*is it really worth it?* Even if
trust is a uniquely human experience, what about ill-founded trust? What
about betrayal?

There's no way to soft-pedal this. Betrayal by someone you trust is a
terrible thing, probably one of the worst experiences a human being can
undergo. One of the most poignant scenes in the fabulous 1995 motion
picture *Braveheart* revolves around just this sort of treachery. The Scottish
patriot William Wallace (Mel Gibson) has been gaining ground against the
British occupation with his makeshift army. He finally gains the support
of the recalcitrant Scottish nobles to fight for their homeland, despite
their ties to Britain. The head of the nobles is Robert the Bruce, who has
pledged his full support to Wallace.

Out on the field of battle Wallace knocks an opposing knight from
his horse. He marches over, victorious, and pulls the helmet off his adversary to discover his identity. To his absolute consternation, Wallace finds
his would-be friend and ally, Robert the Bruce, fighting against him. The
look on Wallace's face is poignant. He becomes dizzy and disoriented,
stumbling about in confusion, no longer sure where he is. The betrayal has
undermined his willpower in a way that no enemy could ever do. It has
utterly deprived him of strength or drive. It is like the experience of Jesus
himself, betrayed by his disciple Judas, or the experience of the psalmist:

> It is not enemies who taunt me—
> > I could bear that;
> it is not adversaries who deal insolently with me—
> > I could hide from them.
> But it is you, my equal,
> > my companion, my familiar friend,

with whom I kept pleasant company;
> we walked in the house of God with the throng.

(Psalm 55:12–14)

So what is the solution? How can we avoid this experience, too painful for words? We have but two choices. Either we can avoid the risk, never allowing anyone to have that power over us, or we can accept the risk, making ourselves vulnerable to just that sort of sorrow. Buddhism opts for the first choice, seeking Nirvana as its ultimate goal. We sometimes think of Nirvana as absolute bliss, a paradise of joy akin to Christian notions of heaven. But this is not the Buddhist idea at all. *Nirvana* is a Sanskrit word that literally means "to cease blowing" and refers to the extinguishing of the passions. It is a peace of soul attained through the suffocation of all desire. Suffering disappears because desire disappears. Utter apathy takes the place of fervent longing and offers the peace of wanting nothing (and getting it). This is one way to achieve serenity. But it is not Christianity.

The person without dreams or aspirations will never experience disappointment, but he or she will also never experience the joy of fulfillment. Jesus trusted and was betrayed again and again. Peter denied him three times, yet after the Resurrection we find Christ again with Peter at his side, confirming him in his mission to feed Christ's sheep and pasture his lambs. Jesus felt abandoned on the cross, but he still prayed, "Father, into your hands I entrust my spirit" (Luke 23:46 GOD'S WORD).

The Christian is told to hope and to dream, to aspire to great things. In fact, he is invited to share in God's own dreams. When God pours out his Spirit, "your sons and your daughters shall prophesy, your old men shall dream dreams, and your young men shall see visions" (Joel 2:28). Paul urges us to "eagerly desire the greater gifts" (1 Cor. 12:31 NIV). Jesus encourages us to ask that we might receive (see Luke 11:9). We are also called to purify our dreams and aspirations so that they correspond to God's dreams for us.

Tennyson wrote "'Tis better to have loved and lost than never to have loved at all." We often forget Tennyson was writing here in *grief* and not in joy; the line that immediately precedes it reads: "I hold it true, whate'er befall; I feel it, when I sorrow most."[3] Tennyson's words are borne out in everyday human experience. No parents who have lost a child wish they'd never had the child in the first place. No wife who has lost a husband wishes she had never married. To love is to risk heartbreak, but even in the heartbreak it is better to have loved.

To love is to expose yourself, make yourself vulnerable, give of yourself, set yourself up for a fall. This is the nature of love. To love is to care, and to care is to put your heart in jeopardy. Trust resembles love, since trust is at the core of what it means to love. And here, 'tis better to have trusted and been betrayed than never to have trusted at all. Or as Samuel Johnson wrote, "It is better to suffer wrong than to do it, and happier to be sometimes cheated than not to trust."[4]

Trusting rightly—where trust is due—is a very good thing. Remember that betrayal is not the only possible outcome. There is also the other side of the coin. To trust and find that trust rewarded with fidelity is one of the most beautiful experiences known to humanity. To trust and be trusted in return, to have confidence in another and find that he or she was worthy of our confidence—this elevates our humanity and binds us to others as no other experience can.

Human trust is rarely total. It exists at different levels and in different degrees. Usually it is partial trust (*I trust my coworker John to replace me at five o'clock*), rather than unqualified trust (*I simply trust Betty*). Partial trust means a willingness to believe that someone will live up to certain expectations in a certain area. You may trust your financial adviser to give you good advice regarding stocks and bonds, but you wouldn't necessarily consult him or her for help in resolving marital problems or recommending medical treatment for your sick mother.

Trust is, in a sense, a *virtue*. The integrity of another person is justly recognized and rewarded with the trust that is due. Yet we should recall what the great Greek philosopher Aristotle said about virtues—they represent a balance between two extremes. Courage, said Aristotle, is the midpoint between the extremes of foolhardiness and cowardice, and the virtue of generosity falls between the opposite excesses of extravagance and stinginess.[5] The case of trust is similar. No one should dispense trust willy-nilly, but neither should we withhold it without cause. Just as a person is innocent until proven guilty, and we would rather let one hundred guilty men go free before condemning one innocent man, so, too, should we offer people the benefit of the doubt. But trust involves courage, as well, since it means exposing ourselves and taking a risk. When we trust another, there is always the chance that the person will fail us. Not only do we risk whatever we have entrusted to him or her; we also risk the pain that his or her betrayal will cause.

What do we risk when we trust? That depends. Some people we trust with little things. We give them some money and ask them to get us a few groceries when they are at the store. Here, the risk is limited to the amount we have entrusted to them. Even if they run off with our hundred dollars, that will be our total loss, and no more. Sometimes we trust others with our secrets, with our inmost thoughts or painful memories. Here, the risk is considerably greater. We have made ourselves vulnerable by sharing things that we would never make public, knowing that the person could publicize them if he or she wanted to. Sometimes we risk more still. Marriage, to take perhaps the best example, means throwing in our lot with another person, binding our life and happiness to his or hers. We trust that our spouse will be faithful, that he or she will love us always, that he or she will be true in good times and in bad. This is exceedingly difficult.

> *I'm kind of ashamed to say it, but at this point in my life I really trust no one. It's not worth it anymore. Too many people have let me down. Too many people have failed me. I've got myself, and that's it.*
>
> —MARTIN, AGE 55

Trust involves belief in the possibility of goodness. We must be open, even inclined to believe in another's goodness in order to trust. Habitual suspicion of others' motives incapacitates a person for authentic trust. We must at times believe they are both willing and able to fulfill what we expect from them.

TRUST AND THE SPIRITUAL LIFE

If trust is essential to our relationship with other people, it is even more so with God. Without trust, we cannot take a single step forward in the spiritual life. Where habitual doubt and distrust make our spiritual lives stagnate, trust is the rich soil in which our spiritual lives flourish.

The Bible holds up the first patriarch—Abraham—as a model of trust. He was the opposite of the worldly, self-made man. He was the God-made man. His belief in God was not theoretical or speculative; it was practical and real. It was faith in action. This was what made him great.

It wasn't easy either. Abraham's trust plays out like a three-part play, each part more dramatic than the last. First God asks Abraham to uproot from his homeland to go to a far-off country that he knew nothing about. His belief in God involved a choice: *Do I go or don't I?* Trusting in God meant a huge sacrifice, that of leaving everything he knew and loved. At seventy-five years of age, Abraham was no spring chicken either, and the move would not have been easy. God didn't even bother telling him where he would go. He said only that Abraham should go "to the land that I will show you" (Gen. 12:1). Abraham didn't know anything about this place; he didn't even know where it was or what would be expected of him when he got there.

Act II. Next, God makes Abraham a promise and wants Abraham to believe in him. He tells Abraham that despite his own advanced age and his wife's barrenness, he will be incredibly fruitful. God takes Abraham outside and says, "Look toward heaven and count the stars, if you are able to count them. . . . So shall your descendants be" (Gen. 15:5). The account goes on to say: "And he believed the LORD; and the LORD reckoned it to him as righteousness" (v. 6). God, who knows the heart of man, knew that Abraham truly believed. He wasn't just saying, "Yeah, right," to God; he trusted in his word and acted on it.

Act III. Finally, God puts Abraham's trust to the test in an even more radical way. After promising Abraham that his progeny would pass through his only son, Isaac, God unexpectedly asks Abraham to sacrifice Isaac to him. Despite the immense pain it causes him, Abraham doesn't waver in his confidence in God. Though he doesn't see or understand, he continues to trust. *God is good. God must know what he is doing.* In the end, Abraham's trust is rewarded. God stays his hand, forbidding Abraham to lay his hand on Isaac.

On considering Abraham's faith in action, the apostle Paul asks an important question: What was gained by Abraham, our ancestor according to the flesh? Was it worthwhile for Abraham to trust God? This is a very good question. If we are to trust in God, is it really worth the effort? And Paul answers that it was Abraham's faith and trust that made him *righteous* before God:

> Hoping against hope, he believed that he would become "the father of many nations," according to what was said, "So numerous shall your descendants be." He did not weaken in faith when he considered his own body, which was already as good as dead (for he was about a hundred years old), or when he considered the barrenness of Sarah's womb. No distrust made him waver concerning the promise of God, but he grew strong in his faith as he gave glory to God, being fully convinced that God was able to do what he had promised. Therefore his faith "was reckoned to him as righteousness." (Romans 4:18–22)

Abraham's biggest gain was not numerous descendants, his new homeland of Canaan, or any other material reward God offered him. Abraham's greatest gain was his own righteousness before God. Trust pleases God like nothing else. It unites us to him and makes love possible.

> *Trust pleases God like nothing else. It unites us to him and makes love possible.*

Since trust is an intimate part of the human experience, it is therefore a part of holiness as well. Holiness makes us more fully human, not less. As Thomas Merton wrote: "[Holiness] is not a matter of being *less* human, but *more* human than other men. This implies a greater capacity for concern, for suffering, for understanding, for sympathy, and also for humor, for joy, for appreciation of the good and beautiful things of life."[6]

Trust in God gives us a sturdiness that no other human security can offer. It gives steadiness, rootedness, stability, and strength. Like a house built on solid rock rather than one built on sand, the person who trusts in God finds in him a firm foundation. He isn't blown about by the winds of fortune but stays strong in both good times and bad. He does not become dejected in adversity or overly inflated in prosperity. As Paul wrote, "Rejoice in hope, be patient in suffering, persevere in prayer" (Rom. 12:12). This trust is beautifully illustrated by a prayer written centuries ago by the great Thomas Aquinas:

> Grant, Lord my God, that I may never fall away in success or in failure; that I may not be prideful in prosperity nor dejected in adversity. Let me rejoice only in what unites us and sorrow only in what separates us. May I strive to please no one or fear to displease anyone except Yourself. May I seek always the things that are eternal and never those that are only temporal. May I shun any joy that is without You and never seek any that is beside You. O Lord, may I delight in any work I do for You and tire of any rest that is apart from You. My God, let me direct my heart towards You, and in my failings, always repent.[7]

In Aquinas's prayer we see that trust in God brings peace of soul. As Isaiah wrote: "One who trusts will not panic" (Isa. 28:16). How often we *do* panic! We are battered about like a little boat on the ocean, victims of the trials and tribulations of our lives. An unshakable confidence in God gives us an interior calm, a refuge against the many storms of our lives. Jesus promises those who follow him a peace "the world cannot give" (John 14:27 NLT). The peace Jesus offers is not a momentary respite in the midst of battle, or a temporary truce in otherwise turbulent times. It is a deep-down serenity that is with us always, a peace that cannot be taken away.

Why are we uneasy? Why are we troubled in spirit? There are surely different causes of our interior unrest. Sometimes we become confused and discouraged because of the evil times in which we live. Sometimes we become troubled and anxious because of our financial situation. Sometimes when we cannot get what we want, we grow frustrated and restless.

Other times still, when others have let us down, we lose our peace of soul. In each of these situations we need the peace that only Jesus can give. This peace is the fruit of our boundless trust in him, and in our confidence that by his side we can never be shaken. He is the friend who will never abandon us.

So trust brings with it righteousness and peace of soul, but this is not all. Trust also allows us to focus on important things, leaving more trivial concerns aside. When our needs are taken care of, we have the necessary time and energy to focus on bigger, more important questions. Jesus advises us to trust in him, to leave our lives in his hands, and to dedicate ourselves to the larger task of preaching his gospel. Look at the way he tells us to prioritize our lives by trusting in the Father's providence:

> Therefore I tell you, do not worry about your life, what you will eat, or about your body, what you will wear. For life is more than food, and the body more than clothing. Consider the ravens: they neither sow nor reap, they have neither storehouse nor barn, and yet God feeds them. Of how much more value are you than the birds! And can any of you by worrying add a single hour to your span of life? If then you are not able to do so small a thing as that, why do you worry about the rest? Consider the lilies, how they grow: they neither toil nor spin; yet I tell you, even Solomon in all his glory was not clothed like one of these. But if God so clothes the grass of the field, which is alive today and tomorrow is thrown into the oven, how much more will he clothe you—you of little faith! And do not keep striving for what you are to eat and what you are to drink, and do not keep worrying. For it is the nations of the world that strive after all these things, and your Father knows that you need them. Instead, strive for his kingdom, and these things will be given to you as well. Do not be afraid, little flock, for it is your Father's good pleasure to give you the kingdom. (Luke 12:22–32)

Our assurance in Christ's ultimate victory over sin and death, and his personal care for us, allows us to work for his kingdom. He carries us in the palm of his hand. With him, we can never lose what is most important. The trusting soul does not fret over material concerns but cares most deeply for what is truly important.

Finally, trust in God is essential for growth in the spiritual life as well. God simply won't have it any other way. God asks us to do impossible things, hurls us into situations that completely surpass our human capabilities, and obliges us either to forge ahead with blind trust in him or to throw in the towel. He does this because he knows that nothing draws us nearer to him than unconditional trust in his unconditional love. He assures us that he is worthy of our trust, the faithful friend who will never leave us destitute. Friends may leave us; comrades may abandon us; even brothers, sisters, parents, and children can betray us, but he never will.

Devotion, intimacy, closeness, and familiarity mark the spiritual life of a soul who truly trusts in God. He is a good Father, loving and provident. Without this trust, how easily our relationship with God becomes characterized by distance, suspicion, legalism, coldness, formality, and withdrawal. There is no intimacy where there is no trust. Trusting souls approach God in prayer, knowing they are heard. Even when they fail to *feel* God in prayer, their faith assures them he is present. Trusting souls ask for more, expect more, dare for more. Their trust confers on them a holy freedom of spirit and a joyful confidence. God is their rock.

You might be thinking, *This is all very beautiful, but is it practical? Is it real? Even when we recognize the splendor and value of trust, is it even possible? How can we really distinguish between a good, wholesome trust and needy dependency, or between healthy trust and gullible stupidity? What sets trust apart and how can we recognize it when we have it?* Let's take a look.

> *Trusting souls ask for more, expect more, dare for more. Their trust confers on them a holy freedom of spirit.*

3

TRUST AND
TRUSTWORTHINESS

When I walk through an art museum I love trying to guess who painted a given work before reading the artist's name. Some artists—like Renoir or Velásquez or Rembrandt—have such distinctive styles that I rarely mistake them for someone else. I may not be able to tell you why (Is it the colors? The forms? The brush strokes? The subject matter? A combination of all of these?), but I nearly always recognize the handiwork.

Trust is a lot like that. You may not know how to define it, but you know it when you see it. Above all, you know it when you *do* it. Trust may look a lot like other experiences—such as faith, hope, expectation, optimism, and reliance—but some essential differences set trust apart. Perhaps the best way, then, to understand trust is by first contrasting it with other attitudes that resemble it.

TRUST VERSUS OPTIMISM

One human attitude that closely resembles trust is *optimism*. It is so close, in fact, that it can easily be confused with the real thing. Optimism is the tendency to always see the bright side of things. As the word implies, it is a matter of *optics*, a prism through which we view reality. By temperamental inclination, the optimist sees the glass as half full while the pessimist sees it as half empty. The optimist is characterized by a buoyancy that minimizes defeats and maximizes victories. This can seem like trust, since an optimistic person always assumes the best of circumstances and people.

There's nothing wrong with optimism, of course. In fact, the Christian faith necessarily breeds a certain optimism, since Christians are not—so to speak—awaiting the final outcome to see "who wins" but harbor the intimate conviction that the final victory has already been achieved in Christ's death and resurrection. Thus, a healthy optimism may even be *related* to our trust in God, while not being the same thing. If we are convinced of Christ's personal love for us and trust in the power of his grace, we cannot help but have a more positive view of life and events than someone for whom the universe is a random and meaningless jumble.

Moreover, our Christian conviction that God is able and willing to bring good even out of evil surely leads to a more positive outlook even of apparently negative happenings. As Paul says, "We know that all things work together for good for those who love God" (Rom. 8:28). This is good grounds for optimism!

But still, optimism and trust are not the same thing. Trust is necessarily and essentially interpersonal. We trust *someone*. Optimism is a habitual way of seeing and interpreting things, which may or may not have anything to do with God or other people. Some are simply optimistic by nature, gifted with a sunny disposition and tending always to expect the best in all circumstances, regardless of the facts. Optimism may even be naive or, worse still, blind in its refusal to consider the negative side of things and persons. Trust, on the other hand, issues from faith in a person who has proven himself worthy of such confidence.

TRUST VERSUS FAITH

We often use *trust* as a synonym for *faith*. To say that we have faith in someone is pretty much indistinguishable from having trust in that person. Yet there is one important difference. Trust implies *risk*. We might believe in another person, but we truly begin to trust only when we go out on a limb. Trust—if you will—is faith in action. It is faith that has taken a step into the dark. Only when something of ours is at stake have we truly begun to trust another.

Unlike mere belief, which may stay at the level of theory, trust shows itself in a willingness to put something precious in someone else's hands. In other words, trusting always involves *entrusting*. It also means having something to lose.

A simple but eloquent example of this is babysitters. Though good babysitters may not hold university degrees or be able to fix a broken carburetor, they all must possess one essential quality: they must be trustworthy. The reason for this is simple. You entrust them with the most precious treasure you have: your children. Babysitters must be responsible enough to take this charge seriously and accomplish it flawlessly. Children are too important to be left in just anyone's care. Trust involves the immense risk of placing your children under someone else's protection. Sure, you will try to minimize the risk—leaving clear instructions, important phone numbers, knowledge of your whereabouts—but in the end the risk is still real, and trust is necessary.

Because it involves risk, trust receives no absolute guarantees. If we were empirically certain that the person we trust could never let us down, it wouldn't be trust anymore. It would be something else. For example, when we don't trust someone, we demand all sorts of conditions. If we lend him money, we ask for collateral. If he promises to deliver something, we require a contract, with legal penalties if he fails to comply. This isn't trust but insurance.

The risk entailed in trust is manifold. Obviously, on one level you risk whatever you have given into another's care. If you lend someone money, trusting him to pay you back, you risk that sum. But on another level you also risk the pain of betrayal, that interpersonal infidelity that can hurt more than the loss itself. You can even risk losing your confidence in humanity, since it is tough to keep trusting when you have been let down again and again.

But like all risk, trust also brings rewards, as we have seen in the last chapter. When trust proves well-founded, the risk pays off and we are confirmed in our belief in another. When another person comes through for us our treasure is safe, and our convictions are bolstered.

This is true in our spiritual lives as well. We can say we *believe* in God (not just that he exists, but that he is worthy of our confidence) but we begin to *trust* God only when we truly lean on him. Trust in God becomes real when we entrust something precious to him.

I've been let down lots of times in life, but I have also known people who were totally true to me. I have had great, loyal friends whom I could completely trust. I think that is what has kept me from becoming a cynic. All it takes is to see that faithfulness is possible, and then you have a reason to believe.

—SHEILA, AGE 60

TRUST VERSUS EXPECTATION OR RELIANCE

A further distinction can be drawn between mere expectation or reliance and true interpersonal trust. We rely on many people and many things. We rely on our cars to start in the morning; we rely on our smoke alarms to go off if there is a fire; we rely on tree branches to hold our weight when we step on them. But in the deepest sense, we don't *trust* these things. We feel angry and disappointed when they fail us, but we do not feel *betrayed*. Betrayal is the experience of another person's failure to come through for us when he could and should have.

Although trust requires expectation (*I expect that the other person will behave in a certain way*), trust and expectation aren't quite the same thing. Expectation expresses a *subjective assurance* that something will happen, without necessarily including interpersonal trust. For instance, I may expect a person to behave in a particular way without trusting him at all. This is because a person may be *predictable* or *reliable* without being trustworthy. We may be able to count on another to react in a determined way (even in a bad way!) without trusting him in the slightest. A person who always acts selfishly may be predictable, since we pretty well know how he will behave in a given circumstance. Still, we do not *trust* this person.

This is the way good detectives operate. They get to know the MO of the criminal they are tracking so as to predict his next move. Unless the criminal is completely erratic, the detectives are able to note preferences and patterns of behavior, and in this way they can foresee how he will operate in the future. But again, this predictability has nothing to do with trust.

Maybe you work for a mean and dishonest manager who would treat you terribly if he could, yet he is restrained by the honest, caring proprietor of the firm, who has forbidden the manager to mistreat you and has asked that you report to him if he does. In this case, the manager may treat you well. You can count on his good treatment, because his fear of censure keeps him in line. Yet you in no way *trust* this person. And if one day he treated you badly, you might feel disappointed, but you would not feel *betrayed*, because you have put no trust in him.

TRUST VERSUS HOPE

Of all its look-alikes, perhaps Christian hope is the virtue that most closely resembles trust. We hope in God because we trust him, and we trust him because we hope in him. Still, hope isn't quite the same thing either, mainly because hope has so many other meanings. For example, one may hope for some*thing*, but one truly trusts some*one*. While hope expresses a *desire* that something will come about, trust expresses a belief about another person. Hope implies a belief in the goodness and faithfulness of another. Therefore, we may *hope* for a raise and *expect* our paycheck, yet we really *trust* only another *person*.

Again, we can see this from the way we react when our hopes are dashed. One who hopes for something (such as a sunny day for a picnic) may feel disappointed or disheartened when it begins to pour rain, but he will not feel *betrayed*. When, however, you place your trust in someone and that person fails you, a feeling of betrayal (and not just disappointment) is inevitable.

Hope can refer simply to an outcome, without any reference to a provider. *I hope to get over my cold before the big meeting on Friday. I hope for a raise. I hope the president appoints a worthy justice to the Supreme Court.* None of these examples of hope involve trust! Let's examine the respective relationship to trust of each of the three examples of levels of hope listed below.

1. SHORT-TERM, MATERIAL HOPES

Sometimes our "hopes" are really just *wishes* expressed as hope. They are desires for future occurrences, without any definite expectation that they will happen. To say "I hope I win at roulette" doesn't express any assurance that I will, in fact, win at roulette, but merely the aspiration to win. Some typical examples of this type of hope (which has little to do with authentic trust!) would be the following:

- I hope I get the job.
- I hope it's sunny this weekend.
- I hope he asks me out.
- I hope she likes me.
- I hope I pass all my exams.
- I hope to live a long life.

2. FEAR DISGUISED AS HOPE

A second category of hopes that still have little to do with trust are those that express fear. In fact, in most of these cases, we could rephrase our hopes as fears. We speak about what we fear might happen in terms of a hope that it will not happen! Some examples of this might be:

- I hope I don't get sick.
- I hope I don't get fired.
- I hope she doesn't find out.
- I hope things don't go wrong.
- I hope the plane doesn't crash.
- I hope it doesn't rain on my day off.

3. AUTHENTICALLY CHRISTIAN HOPE

Real Christian hope differs from these previous examples in two essential ways and is much closer to trust. First, in terms of content, Christian hope is generally directed less toward superficial and material things, and more toward deeper, spiritual goods. So Christian hope is more spiritual, more eternal, more others-centered than secular hope.

Second, Christian hope is not a vague desire for something to happen (or not to happen), but confidence in God. It is based on trust in God—his love, power, and faithfulness. I think you'll see the difference right away from these examples:

- I hope he straightens out his life.
- I hope she is reconciled with her mother.
- I hope this project helps many people discover meaning in their lives.
- I hope my work today pleases God.
- I hope to overcome my vices and grow in virtue.
- I hope everyone I know is saved and reaches eternal life.
- I hope God gives me the grace and strength I need to do the right thing, as well as the wisdom to say the right thing.

It's true that some of these examples could simply reflect a wish or a desire, but if they are expressions of Christian hope, then they also imply a trust in God's assistance. We don't just hope that things happen, we hope in God to let them come about. In a sense, these expressions of Christian hope mirror the Lord's Prayer: "Thy kingdom come. Thy will be done in earth, as it is in heaven" (Matt. 6:10 KJV). It is a desire, but also a request, based on God's goodness and power to fulfill it.

Since trust is essentially interpersonal, it requires a belief about

> *I don't trust many people, but the ones I trust, I trust completely: my dad, my brother Matt, my best friend, Sarah, and a couple others. It's funny because I don't feel a need to have lots of people to trust. I'm happy with the ones I have.*
>
> —GREG, AGE 25

the other person. If trust is well-founded, it means that the other person is worthy of the confidence we place in him or her. We have seen that mere reliability or predictability is not enough to merit true trust. But if not these qualities, what are the essential elements of trustworthiness?

THE FLIP SIDE OF TRUST

As important as trust is, it needs to be earned. There is nothing praiseworthy about trusting foolishly when we have no reason to do so. Though it is always preferable to expect the best of others rather than the worst, our trust should be judicious, not naive. But how do we know who, when, and where to trust? Trust should be dispensed to the trustworthy. This seems like a tautology, and in a way it is. Trust is to *trustworthy* what love is to *lovable* or faith is to *faithful*. It corresponds. The two go together. So in doling out our trust the key questions become: who is trustworthy, and how can we recognize trustworthiness when we see it?

Trustworthiness—like its close cousin, faithfulness—is a *virtue*, or an amalgamation of virtues. It is a moral quality. It is a habitual way of being, a permanent facet of a person's moral character, and not just a spur-of-the-moment action. As we infer from its name, it literally means "worthy of trust" and describes someone who will not let you down. Like the virtue of friendship, trustworthiness is not self-interested but takes on the good of another as its own good and defends it, protects it, and looks to further it.

Since trustworthiness is a virtue that entails an ensemble of different qualities, we can break it down into its component parts. Where all these parts are found, we can be fairly certain we are dealing with a trustworthy person. We will know where to place our trust. Once we have done this, we will be equipped to look at candidates to receive our trust.

COMPETENCE

A key component of trustworthiness is *competence*. You dare to entrust what is valuable to you only to a person who is able to carry out what he proposes. There are plenty of dreamers who sincerely intend what they promise, but who have no way of accomplishing it. You will trust your broken television set to a trained repairman, rather than to a well-meaning neighbor who knows nothing about electricity. You wouldn't hire a mountain guide who has no knowledge of the trails. You wouldn't entrust your child to a nanny who is dizzy and forgetful. Despite their good intentions, such people are not worthy of your trust.

Competence refers to a person's ability to perform the actions you expect from him. This competence is probably limited to a certain realm (such as TV repair or mountain guiding). Since trust involves risk, you don't want to risk something valuable unless you have a reasonable degree of certainty that it will be okay. You don't entrust your secrets to a blabbermouth (incapable of keeping his or her mouth shut), and you don't entrust an important task to someone who is unable to perform it (his incompetence outweighs his goodwill). Without the requisite competence, our trust in others is ill-founded.

As an indication of trustworthiness competence is important, but it isn't enough. It is insufficient for two very important reasons. First of all, a person may be competent but dishonest. You may entrust your broken television to a dishonest repairman who sells it rather than repairs it (though he could repair it if he wanted!). You may enlist a guide with all the right degrees and credentials, only to find that he is a crook. Obviously, something more than competence is needed to make a person trustworthy.

Moreover, a lack of expertise does not make a person completely *untrustworthy* either. I doubt I trust anyone in the world more than my mom and dad, but their technical expertise is not universal and all-encompassing. They are wise and have great stores of common sense, but they have limited knowledge of medicine, finance, astronomy, Chinese history, and constitutional law—to name just a few areas. Yet as real as these limitations are, I wouldn't think of calling my parents "untrustworthy." I may not go to them for lessons in neuroscience, but I would trust them with my life.

Here we can adopt a useful distinction between what Nancy Nyquist Potter refers to as "full trustworthiness" as opposed to "specific trustworthiness."[1] "Full trustworthiness" expresses an overarching moral quality of the person himself, rather than a specific sphere of competence that delineates a particular domain of trust. My parents may not have 100 percent *specific* trustworthiness in all areas, but they have won my full trust. This leads us to the second quality that merits trust.

Goodwill

Perhaps the most essential element of trustworthiness is goodwill. The truly trustworthy person acts not out of self-interest, but out of benevolence toward another. He seeks the other's good rather than his own. If another person acts purely out of self-interest, this may for a time coincide with my best interests, but there are no guarantees. I may hire a lawyer who will work hard for me, not because he really cares about me or my concerns, but because he values his own reputation and wishes to keep me as a client. Recognizing this, I may have a working relationship with the lawyer, but not a relationship of *trust*.

The 1947 film *Miracle on 34th Street* illustrates this beautifully. You may recall that in this movie a man named Kris Kringle starts working at Macy's during the Christmas season, dressing as Santa Claus and greeting children and potential customers at his post at the front of the store. Rather than offer a hard sell for customers to shop at Macy's, Kris starts handing out shopping advice to help buyers get the best deals. He advises one woman to go to Schoenfeld's to buy a fire engine for her son, and he tells another woman that she can find better skates for her daughter at Gimbel's department store—the archrival of Macy's.

At first Kris's employers are irate, since they had instructed Kris to steer parents toward products that Macy's wanted to sell. Little by little, however, they come to see Kris's actions as good for the company, when a woman shopper tells the head of the toy department that she will become a loyal Macy's patron because of its willingness to send people to find better deals elsewhere.

In the end, Kris Kringle's behavior coincides with his employers' strategy. Yet when we compare the self-interest of the Macy's managers with Kris Kringle's genuine goodwill, we see an essential difference. In the end, they agree on the same conduct, but for completely different reasons. The employers do so only to advance sales at Macy's, whereas Kris Kringle does so out of a sincere intent to help customers get the most for their money. As far as trustworthiness goes, we can distinguish between the goodwill of Kris (which rightly inspires and merits trust) and the self-interest of the managers (who would just as easily cheat their customers, if this would increase sales). Goodwill tips the balance between trustworthiness and untrustworthiness.

TRUTHFULNESS

Yet another key element of trustworthiness is *honesty*. We trust people who tell the truth and distrust liars. A dishonest person may make promises that he has no intention of keeping, whereas an honest person tells you the way things are and makes only promises he intends to fulfill.

Earlier we mentioned that we would be unwise to entrust the repair of a broken television to a well-meaning neighbor without the needed skills. In fact, truly trustworthy people wouldn't even *accept* such trust, since they don't make promises that they cannot keep. A trustworthy person wouldn't offer to fix your TV if he wasn't sure he could. A trustworthy person wouldn't hire himself out as a guide unless he was competent to do so. A trustworthy person wouldn't offer to take you home if he didn't know how to drive or was incapacitated. Honesty itself requires a certain degree of humility to admit the limits of one's competence and to promise only what one can successfully carry out.

People with this degree of honesty become trustworthy in a deeper way. We not only trust them in their areas of expertise; we also trust them to tell us if something is too big for them. They won't fudge and tell us they can do something they cannot. They protect our interests by accepting only a trust that is well placed.

MORAL INTEGRITY

The quality of honesty goes hand in hand with another essential trait of trustworthy people. They have *personal integrity* and are faithful to their own principles. A person without principles can never be trustworthy in any true sense; he can be bought or sold. A person of integrity can be counted on to act consistently with his code of ethics.

Even in the absence of personal goodwill, moral integrity can sometimes be sufficient cause to trust in another. A person may not care particularly about you as an individual; he may not even *know* you, but if he has integrity, he will be fair, honest, and responsible in dealing with you. On a good recommendation we could trust another person whom we've never even met, as long as we know that he or she is an upright person of integrity. Like trustworthiness itself, moral integrity comprises several virtues, the most central of which is consistency with moral principle.

Integrity must be proven over time. We've all heard of the so-called "reformed" con man, the one who cajoles and swears that he may have had his slipups in the past, but with you it's different. He really means it now. He's seen the error of his ways. Better yet, *you* have changed him, and he could never let *you* down the way he let others down before you. How many broken hearts and ruined businesses have started out in just this way! Real integrity does not sprout up like a dandelion from one minute to the next. Like a massive redwood tree, it grows strong and solid over time.

Moreover, true moral integrity does not come and go depending on whom we are dealing with. Someone who is trustworthy with some and not with others is ultimately not trustworthy. This is like the proverbial *codice d'onore* of the Sicilian Mafia, whereby one is faithful to members of the *family* but unscrupulous and even vicious with those outside. Here no real moral integrity exists. All it takes is for the parameters to change (you're evicted from the family), and the guy who was your best friend yesterday will gladly stab you in the back today.

Having looked at the qualities that make a person trustworthy, we are ready to start searching for candidates to receive our trust. Above all, we want to know whether God fits the bill. But before we look at God's trustworthiness, we should check out the competition. If not in God, in whom (or in what) will we trust? Let's see how God's rivals stand up to the task.

LEAN
ON
ME

4

GOD'S RIVALS FOR OUR TRUST

Let's say you have saved up twenty thousand dollars and are trying to figure out where to deposit it. What do you do? You may just put it in the local bank, where your parents and grandparents have their bank accounts. It is close by and convenient, and maybe you even know the manager and some of the tellers. You can make a modest return and enjoy reasonable security.

But perhaps you are new in town or simply want to make a more responsible choice. You wonder, for instance, whether you might be able to get a better return elsewhere. What then? You probably analyze a number of important factors. What interest rate does the bank pay on savings deposits? Does it have money market accounts? How about IRAs? What fees apply? Does it offer checking services on savings accounts? How about online banking? And of course you will want to know whether the institution is FDIC-insured.

In the end, most banks are quite similar. Since banking is a regulated industry with a fair amount of competition, you can be reasonably certain that your money is safe and that various banks will give you similar services. The point is, however, that you want to be responsible and do your homework before entrusting your savings to an institution. You look for a trustworthy bank that will be able to defend your assets, offer insurance, and demonstrate goodwill. You must be convinced that its staff will not cheat you but will seek to advance your profits, and that their financial advice will be sound and in your best interests.

Trusting our money to banks is one thing, but our lives are worth much more than our money. Whom do we trust for our emotional, psychological, intellectual, physical, and spiritual well-being? Of all the many candidates for our trust, is God the best choice?

WHOM SHOULD WE TRUST?

If we realize that no man is an island, and that in the end all of us must trust in someone or something, the question becomes: *whom should we trust?* There are many aspirants for the job of savior in today's world, and God is not alone in vying for our confidence. Many prospective candidates compete for the honor of being the rock upon which we can build our lives, and each seeks to convince us that he or she alone is worthy of our trust and devotion. Each promises something different, though in the end they all want us to believe that through them we will find the happiness and security we are looking for. Look at what one typical young person had to say:

In social studies we learned that there are many different religions in the world and no one is really sure who's right and who's wrong. I figure I should stick with something we all agree on, like science or the economy. After that, it's anybody's guess.

—RAYMOND, AGE 16

If you've ever seen Disney's animated rendition of the Rudyard Kipling classic *The Jungle Book*, you undoubtedly recall the memorable character Kaa, a lisping serpent who tries in vain to have young Mowgli for lunch. Besides his treacherous coils, Kaa's principal weapon is his ability to mesmerize his victims. At one point in the film he gazes at Mowgli with hypnotic, spinning eyes and softly sings, "Trust in me," until Mowgli falls into a stupor. This is the way I imagine the many rival candidates for our confidence. They seek to lull us into a false sense of security, only to devour us once we have given in to their intoxicating charms.

God should not be a last resort for our trust, and we shouldn't turn to him just because there is no one else to turn to. We should trust in him because he is faithful and fully deserving of our trust. At the same time, it helps to realize that no one else can guarantee what God guarantees. When we come to understand that many of those who promise us health and happiness are nothing but frauds and charlatans, it is easier to give ourselves over to God.

The Bible has many ways of referring to those who promise much and deliver little or nothing: "[wolves] disguised as sheep" (Matt. 7:15 GOD'S WORD), "false prophets" (Matt. 24:11), and "impostors" (2 Tim. 3:13). But I think my favorite description is the one we find in the book written by the prophet Jeremiah. He describes our false sources of security as "broken cisterns" (2:13 NIV) that hold no water.

BROKEN CISTERNS

These are Jeremiah's words:

> Once more I accuse you, says the LORD,
>   and I accuse your children's children. . . .
> My people have changed their glory
>   for something that does not profit.
> Be appalled, O heavens, at this,
>   be shocked, be utterly desolate, says the LORD,
> for my people have committed two evils:
>   they have forsaken me,
> the fountain of living water,
>   and dug out cisterns for themselves,
>   cracked cisterns that can hold no water.
>
> (Jeremiah 2:9, 11–13)

In the days of ancient Israel, one of the first things a people did on inhabiting a new land was erect towers and dig cisterns—reservoirs to collect rainwater so that the people would always have clean water to drink. These were essential for the life of the people, since water was the most precious commodity in the desert. People needed to know that they would always be able to find this water when they needed it. A broken or cracked cistern proved an immense problem, since all the rainwater collected there would seep out. A cracked cistern was a dry reservoir, a false promise, an empty mirage.

The Lord points out that his people have left him—the true source of living water—and traded him for fraudulent springs of water that cannot fulfill their word. These "idols," these false gods, cannot protect Israel and are not worthy of Israel's trust.

Jesus employs a similar image in John's Gospel account of his meeting with the Samaritan woman at the well in Sychar (see John 4). There Jesus says to her, referring to the water of Jacob's well, "Everyone who drinks of this water will be thirsty again, but those who drink of the water that I will give them will never be thirsty. The water that I will give will become in them a spring of water gushing up to eternal life" (vv. 13–14).

Jesus contrasts the temporary nature of the water of Jacob's well with the renewable, "living" water that he promises. The natural water of the well may quench a person's thirst for the moment, but soon he will grow thirsty again and have to return. This is the best we can hope for from the many earthly competitors for our trust. They may fill us for a moment, entertain us for a time, but eventually they all must prove unfaithful.

IF YOU CAN'T TRUST YOUR OWN MOTHER . . .
(WHOM CAN YOU TRUST?)

In the book of the prophet Isaiah we find an even more striking comparison. There God compares his own faithfulness with that of a mother and makes the bold claim that he is more faithful even than she. We naturally think of our own mothers as the most trustworthy persons on earth.

Speaking for myself, I know that my mother could never betray me, abandon me, or seek anything but my best interests. I trust in her totally. Yet God asserts that his faithfulness is even greater than hers.

The Lord comforts and consoles us much as a mother comforts her child. In his arms we find security and peace, knowing that nothing evil can befall us while he holds us:

> Thus says the LORD:
> I will extend prosperity to her like a river,
>> and the wealth of the nations like an overflowing stream;
> and you shall nurse and be carried on her arm,
>> and dandled on her knees.
> As a mother comforts her child,
>> so I will comfort you;
>> you shall be comforted in Jerusalem.
>
> (Isaiah 66:12–13)

And to those who would feel abandoned or doubt God's providential care, he employs a similar image. He insists that his faithful love exceeds even that of our own mothers. Though we cannot imagine our mothers doing us harm, even if they should fail, he will never fail us. Even if they should forget, he will never forget.

> Zion said, "The LORD has forsaken me,
>> my Lord has forgotten me."
> Can a woman forget her nursing child,
>> or show no compassion for the child of her womb?
> Even these may forget,
>> yet I will not forget you.
> See, I have inscribed you on the palms of my hands;
>> your walls are continually before me.
>
> (Isaiah 49:14–16)

I know I should trust God but I find it really tough. God is supposed to be a good and loving Father, but I have trouble identifying with that. My father was an odious man, and the word father *only conjures up for me horrible memories of abuse and neglect. I want to believe. I really do. Maybe the Holy Spirit will heal me of this one day, but it is such a struggle.*

—ANNE, AGE 31

Here, unfortunately, we cannot help but think of the tragic reality of abortion, where many mothers do, in fact, forsake the children within their wombs. What seemed to the Israelites too terrible to imagine is now a frightfully common reality in our world. And yet again God insists, "Even these may forget, yet I will not forget you."

GOD'S COMPETITORS

So who or what are these "cracked cisterns" that hold no water? Who or what are these rivals for our trust that compete with God? For each of us they may be different things. We all need someone, or something, to lean on. We have to place our security somewhere. And even for those of us who say that all our trust is in God, it is worthwhile to examine our consciences to see whether from time to time we don't allow other false securities to take his place.

Without wishing to be exhaustive in my list of possible competitors for our trust, I could comment on a few that seem fairly typical.

EDUCATION

For some, it is their *education* that makes them feel secure. People who hold degrees and are competent in their fields often feel their knowledge protects them from difficulties others face. They can get a job, so their employment security is all but guaranteed. They feel comfortable around other people in the assurance that they are just as smart, if not smarter, than they are. In fact, education can confer a feeling of superiority over others, even a feeling of being invincible.

While a very good thing in itself, education cannot provide for people when they are sick, or when a spouse walks out. What strength or consolation can education bring when a child dies, or when we reach the age where our future looks short and uncertain?

WEALTH

For others, it is wealth that poses the greatest challenge to God's position as the best recipient of our trust. We will have the chance to explore this topic in greater depth further on, so suffice it to say that this was a rival for our trust that Jesus dealt with on a number of occasions, in the strongest of terms. Money seems to offer the most significant opposition to Christ's lordship in our lives. In our world, money really does talk, and a person of means can get nearly anything he wants. It is easy to understand how the rich can feel omnipotent and self-sufficient and feel less need for God's care and assistance. If the experience of poverty obliges us to trust, then the experience of wealth has the opposite effect.

Wealth may ease our pains and assure some level of comfort in this life, but at the end we know we all will face death as poor persons, with nothing but our character, our personal history, our faith, and our love.

OUR NETWORKS

Another competitor for our trust is our connections, our ability to network, and our power of persuasion. Like material wealth, a web of powerful friends and colleagues can give us a false sense of security. We always have someone to call, someone to turn to, favors to collect, and helpers to enlist for our causes. And even when some of these abandon us, we know that our social graces will allow us to make more friends to take their places.

Some are convinced that all it takes to move up in the world are the right contacts and the right recommendations. "Who you know" can even become more important in many people's minds than "who you are" as a person. I know people who invest untold energy trying to get in with the right crowd and meet the right people, in the hope that this will secure a bright future.

Though one day these friends are bound to fail us (if nothing else, because they are mortal and vulnerable as we are), in the short term they provide a security net that seems to shield us from many of life's woes.

But here, too, a long, hard look at reality leads to the necessary conclusion that friends are great blessings, but poor saviors. They cannot provide the eternal certainty we long for.

INGENUITY

For others, ingenuity and know-how are what most threaten to take God's place as the worthiest candidate for trust. There are those who possess an almost catlike ability to always land on their feet, no matter what the circumstances. After experiencing this a number of times, such people begin to rely more and more on themselves and less on God, convinced that nothing can harm them.

Our personal successes can make us think we have no need of God. It seems we can go it alone. We start believing that we are the sources of our own fortune. Yet in the end, this, too, will fail. We cannot talk our way out of death. The wisdom of the Lord stated in Jeremiah 17:5–7 that cursed is the man who trusts in flesh and blessed is the man who trusts in God will find confirmation in the foolhardy people for whom personal ingenuity acts as a panacea for all ills, and a key that opens every door. Someday that know-how will be tested beyond its strength, and then where will those people look for refuge?

IDEOLOGIES AND THEORIES

For still others, God's rivals are more theoretical abstractions like science, progress, evolution, or politics. When people put their trust in such ideologies or mental constructs that promise to solve all their problems and answer all their questions, they set themselves up for certain disillusion and loss. Science, of course, is a good thing, but like many good things it becomes destructive when taken to an extreme or asked to play a role it cannot possibly perform.

Science, and its more practical form as technology, reveals the beauty of the human intellect and its ability to know and master nature. But science is a mercenary, rather than a true *friend*, and can as easily be used to subjugate man as to liberate him. Just as smallpox vaccinations and motorcars are the fruit of man's scientific prowess, so, too, are the hydrogen bomb and chimeras, and we should think twice before placing our souls under the care of science. Science does not and cannot answer life's most important questions, the hows and whys that determine the meaning of our efforts, our trials, our joys, and our labors.

These few examples do not nearly exhaust the possible rivals for our trust. We have not mentioned, for example, the idol of power—whether military might or the social, political, or intellectual influence exercised by those who have the upper hand over others. Nor have we discussed those optimists who simply resign themselves to the winds of fortune, convinced of their own good luck or ready to play whatever hand is dealt to them. And of course we haven't scratched the surface of the problems of the many who entrust themselves to superstitions such as horoscopes or seek refuge in the escapism of drugs, sex, or incessant noise.

What we have been able to ascertain, I hope, is that none of these false gods can possibly perform the function assigned to them when people place in them their ultimate hope and confidence. In the final analysis, our trust must be in someone or something that is stronger than death and extends beyond the grave; otherwise, the recipient of our trust can promise no more than some unspecified number of years of merriment, after which will come the uncertain moment of complete dissolution or a frightening rendering of accounts. It must be something real and solid, something true and faithful, and not a capricious ally that would just as soon abandon us when a better offer comes along. Moreover, the object of our unconditional trust must be incorruptible and devoted to our ultimate good. If it is itself vulnerable to failure and decomposition, it will be no more enduring and stable than we ourselves.

The necessary question that now presents itself is whether the biblical God and his Son, Jesus Christ, can fulfill this role. Is God up to the task of being our ultimate rock and refuge? Can we trust in him completely? Let's investigate.

5

IS GOD UP TO THE TASK?

The real question this book seeks to answer is: Of all the people or things that could be the object of our trust, why God? Why should we prefer God rather than anyone else? What makes God uniquely special?

Some today would assert that God is the *worst* possible candidate for our trust. You may be aware of how the evolutionary biologist Richard Dawkins describes the God of the Bible. He pulls no punches in his evident disdain for God. According to Dawkins, the biblical divinity "is arguably the most unpleasant character in all fiction: jealous and proud of it; a petty, unjust, unforgiving control-freak; a vindictive, bloodthirsty ethnic cleanser; a misogynistic, homophobic, racist, infanticidal, genocidal, filicidal, pestilential, megalomaniacal, sadomasochistic, capriciously malevolent bully."[1]

Fortunately for Dawkins, God does not exist, so he will never have to come face-to-face with this "bully." As a committed atheist, Dawkins has no use for God and prefers to place his trust in science, even if in the end science will sit by and watch him die as he passes into nothingness. For atheists, the option of trust in God doesn't exist, since God doesn't exist. They have no choice but to look elsewhere.

But what about us believers? Or what about those who aren't convinced one way or the other concerning God? To get a decent idea of God's suitability, we need to go back to the components of trustworthiness we discussed in chapter 3. There we observed that competence, goodwill, truthfulness, and moral integrity are all essential elements of trustworthiness. Perhaps it comes as no surprise that if we evaluate God by these standards, he stacks up pretty well. In fact, he stacks up so well that in the end he seems to be more worthy of our trust than any other, hands down. Let's look for a moment at why this is so.

I doubt very much that God exists. If he did, the world would be a nicer place. When I look around me, I don't see the hand of a loving God but [instead] chaos and confusion.

—SEBASTIAN, AGE 26

GOD'S COMPETENCE

Without wanting to put too fine a point on it, God is the competent one par excellence. He is infinitely more competent than any other being, and God is not just a specialist either, proficient in one area and inept in others. His competence extends to all areas of human existence and beyond. The word we generally use for this is *omnipotence*—the quality of being all-powerful. This means there is literally nothing he cannot do. Nothing baffles him; nothing outwits him; nothing surpasses him; nothing surprises him. We never find God scratching his head and saying, "Gee, I never thought of that." We never find him stymied, standing powerless before an obstacle, wondering how he will possibly overcome it. This is what we mean when we say that God is almighty: there is nothing he cannot do. Or in the words of Scripture, "For God *all* things are possible" (Matt. 19:26, emphasis added).

In the Apostles' Creed we profess that God is the Creator of heaven and earth and all things, visible and invisible. We believe he is eternal, having existed before anything else came to be. We believe that he is omniscient— knowing all things that are, that were, and that will be. The one certain conclusion we should draw from all this is that he is infinitely *competent*.

You may think, *That's fine for creating the universe and saving the world and solving all sorts of big issues of humanity, but what about my little world? What can God do to solve my problems?*

Answer: God's power extends even to the real difficulties that each of us faces. True competence extends from the biggest problems to the smallest details, and that is what we see in God. Jesus said that God was aware of every sparrow that falls to the ground and has counted every hair on our heads (see Matt. 10:29–30). The biblical God doesn't sit in some ivory tower, blithely unaware of the minutiae of our lives. No. What is true of God's competence in running the universe is equally true concerning our lives and problems.

Maybe the most important—and certainly the most consoling—aspect of God's competence is his ability to correct things that have gone sour. We believe that God can right wrongs, undo evils, and make everything all right. No one else can make that claim. He can take the messes of our lives and turn them into something beautiful. It is true, as the nursery rhyme asserts, that "all the king's horses and all the king's men couldn't put Humpty together again." Yet God can. He picks up the pieces of our fragmented existence and doesn't merely glue them back together. He remakes us. Like a shattered sword that is recast in the furnace, we are refashioned in the furnace of his love.

You have probably witnessed those clever artists who ask little children to make squiggles on a sheet of white paper. The artist surveys the squiggle for a moment and then begins to draw around it, incorporating the meaningless lines into an integrated and harmonious whole. In the end, a masterpiece emerges, yet we can still discern the original childish scribbles, which somehow the artist has brought into the new work of art. I imagine that God does something like that with our lives. Though they may look like those childish squiggles, without beauty or order, somehow he is able to make them not only all right, but a veritable masterpiece.

One of the most important lessons of the Cross is that God's power extends to the unthinkable: he is able to bring good out of evil. We must ask ourselves: *If God is able to take the worst evil of all human history—the murder of his Son—and turn it into the means of our salvation, what can he not do with my life? What have I broken that he cannot repair? What have I ruined that he cannot fix? What have I sullied that he cannot make glorious?*

GOD'S GOODWILL

Yet God's competence is not reason enough to trust in him. It is not sufficient that God *can* do all things, that nothing can stand in his way. He must *want* to do all those good things. If we are to trust in him, he must will our good and only our good. And yet here, too, in this essential component of trustworthiness—*goodwill*—God again passes with the highest marks. His goodwill toward us is supreme and unwavering. He cannot will evil. He desires only our good. Even when we turn our backs on him, he perseveres in loving us. More than any mother or father, God sincerely acts in every moment in our best interests. He doesn't abandon us or let us down because of a prior commitment to someone else. God is incapable of betrayal.

God's goodwill isn't reserved for his special little friends but withheld from the rest of humanity. This is why Jesus describes his Father as one who makes "his sun rise on the evil and on the good" (Matt. 5:45), who "is kind to the ungrateful and the wicked" (Luke 6:35), because he does not desire the death of the wicked, but that "they turn from their ways and live" (Ezek. 33:11 NIV). God is not merely just, and he does not treat us as we deserve (thank God!). He treats us infinitely *better* than we deserve. None of us— even the best—deserve his love or goodwill. It is a freely given gift.

The greatest proof of God's goodwill is his willingness to give us his Son, his very life, to be our redeemer. "God so loved the world that he gave his only Son, so that everyone who believes in him may not perish but may have eternal life. Indeed, God did not send the Son into the world to condemn the world, but in order that the world might be saved through him" (John 3:16–17). There was no other reason for Christ to become man, no possible advantage for God except our salvation. God is truly the persistent lover, the stubborn lover, for whom no sacrifice is too great to show his love for us, his beloved.

Some people sincerely wonder how they can trust God after they have offended him. Since they are no longer worthy of his love or goodwill, why should they continue to expect it? The problem here is deeper than we may think and extends to our idea of God's love. People who reason this way (*God can't love me anymore since I'm no longer worthy*) implicitly think that they earlier *were worthy* of God's love. After all, what has changed? They think God loved them because somehow they deserved it. This couldn't be further from the Christian understanding of God.

While it's true that God may have "no good reason" to love me because

I am such a sinner, it's also true that he had no good reason to love me before I offended him either. The reason for God's love is found not in us but in God. We do not earn God's benevolence. We do not merit his passionate love for us. By the same token, neither do we lose it by our sins. We will look at this idea in greater depth further along; for now let it suffice to say that God's goodwill toward us is unswerving and unconditional. He has no interest other than *our* interest.

GOD'S TRUTHFULNESS

What more could we ask of God than his competence and his goodwill? We must ask that he be truthful. As we will see further along, God is truth itself, incapable of lying. He cannot contradict himself. Jesus called himself "the truth" (John 14:6) and challenged the Jewish leaders: "Which of you convicts me of sin? If I tell the truth, why do you not believe me?" (John 8:46). No one can trap him in a lie, because he always speaks the truth. Moreover, as he said to Pontius Pilate: "For this I was born, and for this I came into the world, to testify to the truth. Everyone who belongs to the truth listens to my voice" (John 18:37).

What does this mean for us, practically? It means that God will not make offers he doesn't intend to fulfill, or promises he doesn't intend to keep. We can trust his word. Yet this doesn't always seem to be the case. Don't plenty of things go wrong for those who love God? Doesn't this contradict his promises to be true to us? Look at what Robert Stofel has to say:

> His promises don't always seem to ring true. When we read these passages, we believe that God means what he says. He will protect us, period. We won't succumb to cancer. We won't have a car wreck, and so forth. But often this is not the case. Do we misunderstand God's protection? Is God two-faced in a world known for its righteousness and evil? Is God offering false hope?[2]

Later we will delve into these questions in detail. We will look at what God promises and what he doesn't promise. Often our feelings of disappointment in God stem from expecting things that he has no intention of giving. We will also explore the experience of feeling let down by God and what that means for our spiritual lives. For the moment, let us say that God's promises are not all brought to completion in this short life. Many of his offers find their fulfillment only in the life to come. Yet many other promises find their fulfillment here, too, and we must consider those more closely.

I appreciate Jesus' truthfulness. I get tired of people lying to me or sugar-coating the truth. I really just want the straight story. Jesus said some tough things about the cross and judgment and a bunch of other stuff, but at least we know where we stand.

—MICHAEL, AGE 35

GOD'S INTEGRITY

Finally, we must consider God's integrity. Along with his goodwill toward us, is he true to himself? Does God exact of himself a standard that gives us certainty of his trustworthiness?

Let us begin with an important line from the apostle Paul. Paul writes that even "if we are faithless, he remains faithful—for he cannot deny himself" (2 Tim. 2:13). God offers a covenant to man, but his faithfulness to his side of the bargain cannot be contingent on our faithfulness. That would make God no truer than we are. God sticks with us because he is true to himself and true to us as well, despite our infidelities. He is the model, the yardstick of all integrity.

The biblical passages attesting to this are far too numerous to list, but I will present a couple to give an idea. The Bible portrays God as unchanging in his rectitude and just in all his works.

> I will proclaim the name of the LORD;
> ascribe greatness to our God!
> The Rock, his work is perfect,
> and all his ways are just.

A faithful God, without deceit,

just and upright is he.

(Deuteronomy 32:3–4)

God knows no deceit, no fluctuation, no moral indecision, no equivocation. He is utterly and completely righteous in all his ways. The psalmist, too, cries out: "The LORD is faithful in all his words, and gracious in all his deeds" (Ps. 145:13). And Paul simply writes: "The Lord is faithful; he will strengthen you and guard you from the evil one" (2 Thess. 3:3). The witness of Scripture is uniform: God is true to his word, true to himself, true to his people.

What we read testified in Scripture we find echoed in our own experience. Speaking for myself, I have always known God to be true. Sometimes he is as gentle as a mother, other times unyielding as steel in his tough love. Yet in all of this he is true. In all of this he is love. Never does he contradict himself, and never does he withdraw his love.

I think we often put impossible demands on God in order to believe in him. What would it take, in fact, to make us truly believe in him and trust him unconditionally? What could he do for us that he has not done? I think sometimes we are like the chief priests who look up at Christ crucified and exclaim: "Let the Messiah, the King of Israel, come down from the cross now, so that we may see and believe" (Mark 15:32). Yet that is the one thing he will not do. He will not withdraw his love.

JESUS' TRUST IN GOD

Perhaps the most radical reason for trusting in God is the example we see in Jesus. Jesus showed us that an absolute trust in God is possible. You might be thinking, *Whoa! But Jesus was God! Of course he trusted him!* Not so fast. Jesus was also a man, and he had to struggle with the same difficulties we face. In fact, as we read in the Letter to the Hebrews: "Although he was a Son, he learned obedience through what he suffered; and having been made perfect, he became the source of eternal salvation for all who obey him" (5:8–9).

Again and again Jesus expresses his boundless confidence in the Father's love. He trusts him truly as a son trusts his good father. Before raising Lazarus from the dead, Jesus lifts his eyes to heaven and prays: "Father, I thank you for having heard me. I knew that you always hear me, but I have said this for the sake of the crowd standing here, so that they may believe that you sent me" (John 11:41–42). He knows that he is always heard. He reveals a heart utterly convinced of the Father's trustworthiness.

Jesus never lost confidence in the Father despite the difficulties of the Father's will. In his fidelity to God, he truly suffered and would have desired for the chalice to pass him by (see Matt. 26:39), but this was not the Father's plan. Yet Jesus did not for this reason doubt the Father's love for him. And even when on the cross he felt abandoned by all, including his Father, he still prayed, "Into your hands I commit my spirit."

And Jesus was vindicated in his trust. In Hebrews, we read something very strange: "In the days of his flesh, Jesus offered up prayers and supplications, with loud cries and tears, to the one who was able to save him from death, and he was heard because of his reverent submission" (5:7). It would seem at first glance that Jesus was not heard; in fact, the one "who was able to save him from death" chose not to do so! In what way was he heard? It seems quite the contrary. Some minutes later soldiers arrived to cart him off to torments and death.

When Abraham was ready to sacrifice Isaac, an angel came and stayed his hand. This never happened with Jesus. No angel appeared. There was no sparing of the punishment. Yet although Jesus passed through death, it had no power to hold him. The Father raised him from the dead. What Jesus prayed for with greatest intensity and in an unqualified way was that the Father's will be done. And he was heard.

Meditating on the mystery of Christ's trust can throw important light on our own trust in God. But now let us look for a moment at what shape this trust should take in our own lives. How are we called to trust, and what will this trust look like in the life of a Christian? How can we resemble Christ in our trust? This will be the subject for our next chapter.

6

WHAT TRUST IN GOD LOOKS LIKE

Like many students of high school French, I was required to read *Le Petit Prince*, a novella by the French writer and aviator Antoine de Saint-Exupéry. The book contained a number of rudimentary illustrations by Saint-Exupéry himself.

Though ostensibly a children's story, *The Little Prince* makes several important points about human existence through the medium of a very simple story line. The narrator tells of meeting a young prince from another planet in the middle of the Sahara Desert. Saint-Exupéry contrasts the innocence and wisdom of childhood with the pseudosophistication of adulthood.

A key character besides the prince himself is a fox the prince meets and tames on his visit to earth. It is the fox who explains the nature of things to the prince through aphorisms, the most famous of which is "*On ne voit bien qu'avec le cœur, l'essentiel est invisible pour les yeux*" (One sees well only with the heart; what is essential is invisible to the eyes). Yet, for me, perhaps the most important line of the book was another, which read: "You become responsible forever for what you have tamed."

This saying struck home with me because I could relate it to my own experience. When I was a young boy I used to style myself something of an animal tamer. Not of lions and tigers, but of simpler woodland creatures. More patient than now, I would sit still for hours in silence, tossing nuts to a squirrel or chunks of bread to a raccoon, hoping to slowly gain its confidence.

I especially remember one squirrel, which I named (unimaginatively) Red. He was a beautiful animal—smallish, red-hued, with a lush, flowing tail and large, black eyes that darted nervously back and forth. Red was especially skittish, even by squirrel standards, and the first few times I saw him, he simply turned tail and ran for cover. I would try to stand stock-still so that he would realize I meant no harm and didn't take a particular interest in him. Eventually, he became somewhat habituated to my presence and would tolerate me as long as I made no sudden moves and didn't attempt to get anywhere near him.

Though it represented a marked improvement over our initial relationship, this arrangement didn't satisfy me. I intended for us to be friends and not merely to put up with each other. The next stage in our rapport consisted of my throwing peanuts over near where Red was foraging for food. Again, at first the brusque movement required in pitching the nuts was enough to send Red bolting. Soon, however, he got used to that as well. To make a long story short (since the process lasted weeks), the nuts gradually found their way nearer and nearer to the thrower. We finally reached the point where Red no longer feared me and would even sit on my knee while I fed him out of my hand. Over the years I repeated the process with other rodents, rabbits, and especially raccoons, with comparable results.

Though the analogy is weak, I imagine that God sometimes has to undertake a similar procedure with us. He tosses us gestures of his love, first at a distance, then nearer to him. And we, like the squirrel, at first run from him, frightened by his intrusions into our safe, controlled world. Later we take the prize he offers—provided that we don't have to get too near to the source. We accept God's gifts but are afraid of what could happen if we allowed him more deeply into our lives. Yet, slowly, we learn to trust the hand that feeds us, to believe in his goodness.

What is taming, after all, if not the process through which we gain another's trust? I'm not really sure which is more difficult, taming, or letting ourselves be tamed. Being "tamed" means overcoming our natural fears and suspicions. It means learning that the other will do us no harm and is worthy of our confidence. And the one who tames becomes responsible for the one tamed.

TRUST IN THE TAMER

It's not only hard to let ourselves be tamed by God, however. It's also hard sometimes to distinguish true trust (the kind that God is looking for) from false trust. Sometimes what we think is trust in God is really something else altogether.

One look-alike that is sometimes mistaken for trust is *presumption*. We sometimes take little care for our choices in the assumption that sins don't really matter. This presumption abuses God's mercy and kindness, in supposing that in the end our actions have no consequences. Like delinquent tenants, we carelessly trash the house in the subjective assurance that God will clean things up.

While God's mercy indeed knows no bounds or limits, it does require a minimum of good faith on our part. Asking his pardon while planning our next crime hardly constitutes an acceptable disposition for receiving God's forgiveness. We must at the very least recognize our sins as sins and be willing to repent of them, or pardon becomes impossible—not because of God's unwillingness to bestow it, but because of our inability to receive it.

Sometimes people presume on their own goodness and personal merits, supposing that they don't need God's mercy. Other times, people presume on God's mercy, expecting to obtain it automatically, despite their obstinacy in sin. Neither one of these squares with authentic trust, which looks to the goodness of God with humility and boundless confidence. Here we must be clear. Presumption is not an *excess* of trust, but a *perversion* of trust. One cannot trust too much in God, but one may trust in the wrong way. While presumption may resemble great trust in God's mercy and love, in reality it puts his mercy and love to the test.

There is a huge difference between *trusting* God and *testing* him. A good example of this can be found in Christ's temptations in the wilderness. There the devil invites Christ to throw himself down from the pinnacle of the temple, in a sense forcing God's hand to save him. And Jesus responds, "You shall not put the Lord your God to the test" (Matt. 4:7 NASB). What the devil proposes as *trust*, Jesus unmasks as a *test*. Testing God means doing things *our* way and expecting him to pick up the pieces and patch things up afterward.[1] Confidence, on the other hand, means uniting ourselves to *God's* plans, knowing that if we do things his way, he will bring everything to a fruitful conclusion.

A second counterfeit that is sometimes confused with trust in God is moral and spiritual *laxity*. This impostor is similar to presumption, in that the lax person assumes that he need do nothing in life to gain salvation. Whereas Christians believe that salvation comes not from human works but from Christ's redemptive sacrifice, we also believe that our free cooperation is needed. God does not impose salvation on us but looks for our goodwill and allows us to accept or reject him.

A lax person minimizes personal responsibility, whereas a trusting person accepts personal responsibility while recognizing his deep need for God's grace. For a morally or spiritually lax person, personal effort is not required. Faith without love suffices. In some cases this laxity rests on a theological error regarding predestination. According to this school, God has already decided who will be saved and who will be condemned, so human freedom is irrelevant—at best a useful fiction. In the end our choices don't matter. This theory flies in the face of Christ's teachings on judgment, which clearly link our eternal reward or punishment with our free decisions. Unlike laxity, trust doesn't try to eliminate personal accountability.

A third counterfeit trust is *superficiality* or spiritual shallowness. Some people don't bother to get to know their faith or practice it with any seriousness. They prefer to leave this to the religion "professionals." If any spiritual thought disturbs their laid-back confidence that everything is fine, they simply dismiss it.

This superficiality may seem like trust, since the serenity and peace of soul that accompany it are similar to those experienced by one who trusts. Yet such shallowness often covers up a deafness to the Holy Spirit's summons to grow in generosity. Real Christian trust goes hand in hand with serious effort. Moreover, it means honest acknowledgment of our sins and neediness, as well as the challenges of the Christian adventure, rather than a cavalier dismissal of personal shortcomings.

Things are very different for one who trusts fully in God. An acknowledgment of personal failings propels the trusting person into the arms of our heavenly Father, rather than making him shrink away in shame and fear. Again Jesus insists: "Fear not!" Yes, our sins and failings are real, but he comes not to condemn but to save. He is the Good Shepherd who binds up the wounded and carries them on his shoulders.

BOUNDLESS TRUST

If these are some of the pitfalls we are to avoid, what does real trust in God look like? How can it be differentiated from simple trust in other people? The most distinctive—and scariest—characteristic of true trust in God is that it should be *total* and *boundless*. We normally trust people and institutions according to their areas of expertise. A biologist might not be sound in responding to ethical questions, any more than a movie star deserves special credibility in political matters, but that's okay as long as they stick to their specialties. Consult actors about acting and biologists about biology and everything's fine. Most people, after all, ask us for partial trust. For example, we may trust our thrice-divorced accountant for tax advice, but we probably wouldn't turn to him to help solve our marital problems. We similarly might have absolute confidence in our Scientologist attorney when it comes to legal advice, but we would think twice before asking him for theological counsel or suggestions to improve our spiritual lives.

This is the difference between partial and total trust, or divided and undivided trust. And where God begs us for undivided trust, we often prefer to give him a portion of our trust. We would like our trust in God to be part of a diversified investment portfolio. Financial planners will counsel us to avoid putting all our eggs in the same basket, in case the market suffers. So we may do the same with our trust in God. Just as an investor may have a little money in the futures market, a larger percentage in stocks, another in bonds, another in a money market, some sitting in the bank, and a few bucks in the cookie jar, we would like to trust in God, but not *only* in God. Let's see . . . 26 percent God, 15 percent my ingenuity and know-how, 19 percent in contacts and references, 12 percent friends, 21 percent family, 4 percent astrology, and 3 percent good luck. For investors, this diversity is supposed to help maximize returns while minimizing risk. We try to spread out our investments to assure the greatest future yield. It also includes a plan B (in case plan A fails). Many times we, too, would like a plan B, in case God fails us (or maybe God is the plan B, if all else fails!).

Depending on where we fall on the risk scale, we may vary our percentages. We can follow the *have your cake and eat it too* strategy, the *middle of the road* strategy, the *self-made man* strategy, or even the *let's wing it* strategy. But God asks for something else. He wants the *all for you* strategy.

The biblical God defines himself as a "jealous God" (Exod. 34:14), and he doesn't take kindly to sharing our allegiance with other "gods." He wants all of our trust. He wants us to trust in him unconditionally, through thick and thin. Jesus tells us that where our hearts are, there our treasures will be also, the original version of "Put your money where your mouth is." He wants our faith and our trust to be the real things, not mere lip service. This undivided trust can be unnerving. But let's face it, God is either totally trustworthy or not trustworthy at all.

In the end, there is something tremendously satisfying about trusting completely in God. When we come to realize that our lives are wholly in his hands, that he is in charge and that he is the Lord of history, an immense weight is lifted from our shoulders. No longer does the buck stop with us. No longer are we the ones who will change the world. It is God.

PRACTICAL TRUST

Our trust in God is not only supposed to be boundless, it is also supposed to be *practical*. That is, it is meant to go beyond pretty theory and nice words. In the Gospels Jesus tells a curious story about two brothers. No, I'm not talking about the well-known story of the prodigal son and his elder brother, but two other brothers (see Matt. 21:28–32). These two brothers had a father who was a vineyard owner.

One morning the father wakes up and tells his first son, "Son, go and work in the vineyard today" (v. 28). The son answers rather rudely, "I will not" (v. 29). Later, however, he thinks better of it, and despite his earlier refusal, he goes out to the vineyard to work. The father also goes to the second son and says the same thing. This son answers much more obediently and respectfully than the first and assures his father that he will go. However, the second son doesn't go after all.

Jesus tells this parable to distinguish between our words and our actions. We may talk a good game, know all the right answers, but never do the right thing. That is, we may be able to recite perfect answers about God and what he expects from us, while never really giving it to him in our day-to-day lives. In the end, Jesus explains, our actions matter more than our words. What we *do* matters much more than what we *say* we will do.

We may say we believe, while in reality we don't rely on God at all. Some people are theoretical believers but practical atheists. If you ask them whether they believe in God, they will tell you they do. But this doesn't show in their choices. In practice, they live as if God didn't exist. They will tell you how important prayer is but rarely or never pray. They will tell you that trust in God is essential, but they never really trust him.

Conversely, there are many people who believe, even though they say they don't. They may say they reject God and religion but live more "religious" lives than many people who profess faith with their lips. This doesn't mean that our words are not important. Jesus enjoins us to stand up and acknowledge him before others (see Luke 12:8–9), and Paul says that our outward profession of faith leads to salvation (see Rom. 10:8–10). What it does mean, however, is that our actions mean even more still! In the end, Jesus says, doing God's will or not doing it is a matter of *action* (see Matt. 7:21–27).

This same principle holds true as far as trust is concerned. Some people say that they trust God, but as soon as some difficulty presents itself, they panic. They

> *In theory I trust in God, but I can't say it comes through in my actions, decisions, or stress management skills.*
>
> —JOCELYN, AGE 40

look for every possible security and turn to God only as a last resort. Their trust goes no further than their lips.

FATHER KNOWS BEST

Another aspect of trusting God consists of relinquishing our hold on things and allowing him to guide us. Letting him be God and letting ourselves be his children means accepting his wisdom and his view of things as the very best for us, even though we don't see how this can possibly be the case. There is nothing harder than letting go of our own opinions and our judgment of how things should be done. Yet God often has other plans. He has his way of doing things, and if we're not flexible, we may find ourselves rebelling against him rather than trusting in him.

Does God really know best? Of course he does. But we often would rather do things our way. Since we cannot see the outcome, we cling to our earthly wisdom rather than step out in an act of true confidence in him. Let's look at how this plays out.

Sometimes my expectations are misguided. Often, there is something that I think would be good for me (i.e., getting into a specific college, dating a particular guy, etc.) and when it doesn't work out, then sometimes my first thought is to doubt God's love for me.

—CAITLIN, AGE 23

At certain times Jesus asked his disciples to do some pretty kooky things. For example, one day Jesus told Simon Peter to go throw a hook into the lake, pull out the first fish that bit, and extract a coin from its mouth (see Matt. 17:27). Now Peter was a more experienced fisherman than Jesus was and could easily have said, "That's insane! You don't just throw a hook into the water, and fish don't have coins in their mouths!" But Peter trusted, so he did what Jesus said.

Another time, Jesus told the waiters at a wedding to fill six enormous jars with water and to take some to the chief steward to taste (see John 2:1–11). Again, a logical response might have been, "Why should we? We don't need water; we need wine. And furthermore, we will lose our jobs and look like fools if we take water to the steward to taste!" But they didn't. They trusted, and their trust was rewarded.

Jesus often asks us to do things that don't seem to make much sense at first. We often scratch our heads, wondering what in the world God is doing in our lives. Things seem to go wrong. Our plans don't work out. Even things that seemed to be God's will all of a sudden get turned on their heads. What's up?

The key here, I think, is to remind ourselves—every day, if necessary—that *God knows what he is doing*. Trust involves not only the big picture, but the nitty-gritty events of our everyday lives. That is where it can be hardest to trust, but also where it is most necessary. It takes humility, but we must recognize that God knows even better than we do what is best for us and for those we love. We need to give him room to work and cooperate with him, rather than resist him.

One thing that can help is to remember that sometimes we have to let things unfold before we discover God's wisdom. A simple story illustrates this nicely. The story has many versions, but the basic gist is the same in all.

Once upon a time, there was a farmer in the central region of China. He didn't have a lot of money, and, instead of a tractor, he used an old horse to plow his field. One afternoon, while working in the field, the horse dropped dead. Everyone in the village said, "Oh, what a horrible thing to happen." The farmer said simply, "We'll see."

He was so at peace and so calm, that everyone in the village got together and, admiring his attitude, gave him a new horse as a gift. People who heard about it exclaimed, "What a lucky man!" And the farmer said, "We'll see."

A couple of days later, the new horse jumped a fence and ran away. The people in the village shook their heads and said, "What an unlucky fellow!" The farmer smiled and said, "We'll see." Eventually, the horse found his way home, and everyone again said, "What a fortunate man." The farmer simply said, "We'll see." Later in the year, the farmer's young boy went out riding on the horse and fell and broke

his leg. Everyone in the village said, "What a shame for the poor boy."
The farmer said, "We'll see."

Two days later, the army came into the village to draft new recruits.
When they saw that the farmer's son had a broken leg, they decided
not to recruit him. Everyone said, "What a fortunate young man." The
farmer smiled again—and said, "We'll see."

The moral of the story is evident. We tend to react strongly to immediate events, as if they tell the whole story. Yet many times what looks like
a setback may actually be a gift in disguise, and vice versa. Trust in God
allows us to accept the many ups and downs in life with the assurance that
he has a bigger plan, and that he knows what he is doing.

TRUSTING GOD MEANS TRUSTING THE CHURCH

After Jesus' resurrection, he appeared to the apostles who were gathered
in the upper room, but, as we know, Thomas was not with them. When
Thomas returned, the others told him the astounding, wonderful news
that Jesus had risen from the dead. Rather than rejoice with them, however,
Thomas resolutely vowed not to believe until he could see for himself. He
said, in fact, that he would never believe until he could put his fingers in
the nailprints in Jesus' hands and place his hand into Jesus' side where the
soldier's lance had pierced it (see John 20:25).

None of us likes secondhand news. We all would like to see for ourselves rather than rely on the testimony of others. Yet God didn't set things
up this way. He intended that some would become the vehicles for others' belief. He appeared to some, made himself known to some, that they
might announce him to the world. The Church's mission is to announce
Christ to the world and to teach in his name. Since the very first century
this is what the Church has done, and it continues to this day.

We know how Thomas's story finished. A week later the apostles were
again in the upper room, and this time Thomas was with them. Despite
the closed doors Jesus came and stood before them once again, and the first

person he addressed himself to was Thomas. "Put your finger here and see my hands," Jesus said. "Reach out your hand and put it in my side. Do not doubt but believe" (John 20:27). The sight of Jesus satisfied Thomas and he declared, "My Lord and my God!" (v. 28).

But Jesus had more to say. "Have you believed because you have seen me? Blessed are those who have not seen and yet have come to believe" (v. 29). For most generations of Christians, the option of withholding belief until we can see Jesus for ourselves does not exist. We must rely on the testimony of his chosen witnesses or refuse to believe. Jesus has called us to be witnesses to one another, to aid each other in belief, and to encourage one another to be faithful. This is why he founded the Church.

Jesus said to his apostles, "The person who hears you hears me, and the person who rejects you rejects me. The person who rejects me rejects the one who sent me" (Luke 10:16 GOD'S WORD). Jesus gave them his own authority and identified himself so closely with them that they were charged to speak in his name. So when Jesus speaks about fraternal correction, he urges his followers to first try to win over the wrongdoer with personal arguments or the witnesses of two or three others, but if this fails, the Christian should refer the matter to the authority of the church. Here's what he says: "If the member refuses to listen to them, tell it to the church; and if the offender refuses to listen even to the church, let such a one be to you as a Gentile and a tax collector. Truly I tell you, whatever you bind on earth will be bound in heaven, and whatever you loose on earth will be loosed in heaven" (Matt. 18:17–18).

And this is the way the Church lived, even early on. Thus, when Paul wrote to the bishop Titus, he enjoined him, "Declare these things; exhort and reprove with all authority" (Titus 2:15). He likewise wrote to the bishop Timothy,

> I solemnly urge you: proclaim the message; be persistent whether the time is favorable or unfavorable; convince, rebuke, and encourage, with the utmost patience in teaching. For the time is coming when people will not put up with sound doctrine, but having itching ears, they will accumulate for themselves teachers to suit their own desires, and will turn away from listening to the truth and wander away to myths. (2 Timothy 4:1–4)

How, we may well ask, should we balance this trust in the Church with the evident failings of so many of her pastors throughout history? Jesus clearly does not prevent his representatives from sinning, so why should we listen to them? Maybe we can get a clue from what Jesus said about the scribes and Pharisees in his day. He said to the crowds and to his disciples, "The scribes and the Pharisees sit on Moses' seat; therefore, do whatever they teach you and follow it; but do not do as they do, for they do not practice what they teach" (Matt. 23:2–3). Here we have the case of people who possess true, God-given authority but are not good role models. One thing Jesus does *not* say is, "If your religious leaders aren't perfect, you have no reason to listen to them." Instead, he advises heeding the leaders' teaching, while disregarding their bad example.

We can see many examples of this in the history of the Christian Church. We have had leaders who were scandalous in their private lives but continued to preserve the deposit of faith in their teaching. For Catholics, one glance at the history of the papacy gives witness to this. Sure we have had many saintly popes, but we have also had popes who gave miserable examples of what it means to be a Christian. Yet, through it all, sound doctrine has been preserved—due not to human genius or perfect people, but simply to God's faithfulness. Christ founded the Church, and he continues to guide and protect it.

In fact, we are called not to trust in God *and* the Church, but to trust in God *through* the Church. The Church wouldn't merit our trust if it weren't for its divine founding and divine protection. Paul called the Church Christ's bride, whom he loved and for whom he gave his life. To love and trust the Church is to trust Christ's spouse. Paul also called the Church Christ's body; the head and the body form one Christ—not two.

Trust in God—real trust—is a beautiful adventure, one that wouldn't be possible without God's grace. It is a gift to be able to trust God in a practical, boundless way. But at the same time, it is also a gift we present *to* God. Let's see how this is so.

7

TRUST AS A GIFT *TO* GOD

We often wonder what benefits trust can bring *us*, but we fail to realize that trust is also a gift we give to *God*. What, after all, do you give a God who has everything? What can we possibly offer him that he doesn't already have? He cannot possibly need our gifts!

Remember God's words as expressed by the psalmist that eloquently reveal the utter superfluity of our gifts and sacrifices to God:

> Not for your sacrifices do I rebuke you;
>> your burnt offerings are continually before me.
> I will not accept a bull from your house,
>> or goats from your folds.
> For every wild animal of the forest is mine,
>> the cattle on a thousand hills.
> I know all the birds of the air,
>> and all that moves in the field is mine.
> If I were hungry, I would not tell you,
>> for the world and all that is in it is mine.
> Do I eat the flesh of bulls,
>> or drink the blood of goats?

(Psalm 50:8–13)

Yet there is one thing that God doesn't have and that he passionately desires: our trust. It seems as if our trust is merely for ourselves, and that is mostly true. When we trust in God, we have everything to gain. At the same time, God hungers and thirsts for our trust. Nothing seems to offend his heart more than our failure to trust in him.

Christians often wonder how they can better love God. We know that Jesus summed up Christian morality in his command to love the Lord our God with all our hearts, all our souls, all our minds, and all our strength, and to love our neighbors as ourselves (see Mark 12:29–31). Now the second part of this—love of neighbor—is relatively straightforward. We know what our neighbor needs. We can come to his or her assistance. We can treat him the way we would like to be treated. But the first part of Jesus' Great Commandment is more complex. When asked what it means to love God with all our hearts and how we are to practice this, we often respond by scratching our heads in befuddlement.

We know *some* answers, to be sure. We know that we express our love for God by praising him, glorifying his name, and singing of his marvelous works. We show our love by thanking him for his gifts. With grateful hearts we acknowledge his benevolence and the bounty of his goodness. Perhaps most important of all, we manifest our love for God by embracing his will in our lives, earnestly trying to live in a way that is pleasing to him. After all, Jesus said, "If you love me, you will keep my commandments" (John 14:15). Our obedience to God's will is a prime way of exercising our love for him.

But there is another beautiful way of expressing our love for God that we probably don't think about enough. When we *trust* in him, we are loving him in return. There is no greater pleasure for one who loves than to be trusted. Think how sad it would be—and, alas, often is—if people whom God passionately loved didn't believe or trust in that love. Think of mothers and fathers who selflessly devote their total existence to their children, only to find that the children doubt their love. Could anything be more tragic and more painful?

It often seems to me that the Bible is simply an extended testimony of God's love for humankind—for you and for me. It is as if he is crying out on every page how much he loves us and begging us to trust in that love.

Through the prophets and kings, through the Psalms and Chronicles, and especially through his only begotten Son, he shouts to us that there is *nothing* he would not do for us, so much does he love us. And in the face of all this, he desires above all a response of trust. He wants us to believe in his love. And when we respond in this way, we become a balm for his heart and a consolation for his wounds of love.

> *I sometimes feel guilty when I realize I haven't trusted in God and then things turn out well. I suppose I should learn from this that he is worthy of my trust all the time. I know it must hurt him when I doubt his love for me.*
>
> —MICHAELA, AGE 13

If we want to love God as we should, there is no better place to start than by trusting him. And if we truly wish to grow in trust, we must likewise strive to avoid sins against trust, anything that can tarnish the trust that he deserves and longs for.

SINS AGAINST TRUST

Many times what seem like normal, "human" reactions to difficulties really reflect a lack of trust in God. Our worries and anxieties, our doubts and fears, our frustrations and complaints, our discouragements and our self-sufficiency—do these not reveal an attitude of distrust in God and his providential love? Of course they aren't always sinful, and many times they are merely spontaneous feelings rather than free choices we make. Still, by calling these attitudes and reactions by their names, we can more consciously work against them, and in this way we may be able to cultivate a more trusting attitude. If we truly wish to love God, an effort to overcome our distrust is fundamental. Let's examine four of these attitudes that can jeopardize our trust in God.

ANXIETY

One of these "natural" reactions to bad news, hard times, or simple uncertainty about the future goes by the name of *anxiety*. Anxiety refers to a distress or uneasiness of mind caused by fear of danger or misfortune. We experience it when our souls are troubled either by real or imagined adversities—anything from final exams to rocky romantic relationships to infirmities. Anxiety is closely related to worry, doubt, and fear. We fret, we doubt, we are afraid and disturbed by what the future may bring. *What will happen to us? Will things turn out all right? Will we clear the next hurdle? How will I go on if such and such happens?*

Again, such sentiments may be nothing more than an impulsive reaction to the thought of possible future troubles. When we foresee hard times, we naturally begin to fear and to become uneasy. Yet here is where trust in God proves so essential. The thought that God loves us, that he is always with us, that he will never let us be tempted beyond our strength, and that any temporal difficulty is by its very nature short-lived when compared to eternity, gives us strength to face our problems with courage and stoutheartedness. An unhesitating belief in God's providential care keeps us from becoming overly worried and preserves our peace of soul.

Doubt, of course, can be either good or bad. We all experience doubt as we mature in the faith. Innocence gives way to a legitimate questioning, which in turn often flowers into a more firmly held belief. It is stubborn doubts, doubts that persist when God has already shown his faithfulness, that begin to undermine our trust and our love. We are all called to pursue truth, and then to cling to it relentlessly when we have found it. God merits our trust, and when we have realized this, we should never return to our doubts.

Fear, too, is a close cousin of anxiety. It also has a positive and negative side. John says that perfect love casts out all fear (see 1 John 4:18), and the same must be true of perfect trust. When we trust totally, what have we left to fear? But the Bible speaks about two different kinds of fear, which Catherine of Siena characterized as "servile fear" and "filial fear."[1] Servile fear—the fear of a slave for his master—is the fear of punishment and of the master himself. A slave knows that the master controls his life and fears that the master may dispose of him in an evil way. A slave mistrusts because a slave is owned as a useful tool and not loved as a child.

Filial fear—the fear felt by a son or a daughter—is different from this.

This is the fear that the Bible describes as "the beginning of wisdom" (Prov. 9:10) and also as a gift of the Holy Spirit. How is this so? In what way does fear of the Lord make us wise? As a virtue, "fear of the Lord" simply means taking God as our point of reference for all our decisions. His pleasure or displeasure with our actions becomes our overriding concern, superior to what others will think or what we may gain or lose by our choices. To fear the Lord is to care above all for him, and to serve no other with the loyalty that he alone deserves.

In this context, we can better understand what the psalmist meant when he wrote, "You who fear the LORD, trust in the LORD! He is their help and their shield" (Ps. 115:11). Here trust is juxtaposed with fear not as its opposite, but as its complement. It is precisely those who fear the Lord (reverence and respect him) who are called to trust in him. Reverence and obedience alone are insufficient. What God wants above all is our trust in him.

Thus the psalmist could further write, "In God I trust; I am not afraid; what can flesh do to me?" (Ps. 56:4). To have God as both our beginning and our end, the one to whom we give everything and from whom we expect everything: this is the essence of the psalmist's message. To fear God is to live for him; to trust in him is to draw every good thing from his providence. The apostle Paul picked up on this very theme when he wrote: "If God is for us, who is against us? He who did not withhold his own Son, but gave him up for all of us, will he not with him also give us everything else?" (Rom. 8:31–32).

COMPLAINT

To complain is human, or at the very least, one would think so from how common it is. I have, however, had the very good fortune of meeting people in my life who never complain. Alas, I am not one of them. I easily express my negative feelings when people let me down, or when things don't go according to my wishes. But I have met people—not many—from whom one never hears a negative word. They seem psychologically incapable of focusing on the negative side of things and instead immediately look to the positive. They never express dissatisfaction or resentment and seem to bear mishaps quite as well as they embrace good fortune.

My biggest fault is that I'm really critical—of myself, of my friends, and even of God. I'd love to learn how to take everything he gives me without complaining, but I always seem to find something wrong with everything.

—BRIAN, AGE 22

The reason I include complaint among the enemies of trust is threefold. First, a complainer (we all know the type I mean) adamantly concentrates on the negative. A complainer seems never satisfied with his or her lot; there is always something missing, something not quite right. This is spiritually problematic because it leads us to minimize the presence of God's grace and love in our lives, to overlook his abundant gifts. Rather than acknowledge his manifest love for us—even in times of trial—we accentuate the difficulties of our existence. All of us have problems, of course, but to complain is to choose to express our sadness and dissatisfaction with the state of things. This corrodes our trust in God and encourages a jaded view of his action in our lives.

Second, complaint in turn is closely allied with ingratitude, since both fail to recognize the cornucopia of gifts that God showers upon us on a daily basis. A habitual dissatisfaction with life cannot coexist with a grateful heart that sees everything as a freely given sign of God's attentive care of his children. A grateful person cannot get over her good fortune at being chosen by God to be the recipient of his love. She acknowledges being unworthy of such gestures, which makes her all the more overwhelmed at receiving them.

If a pauper were offered a room in the king's castle, I doubt very much that he would complain about the furnishings or color scheme! Gratitude begets trust, since it focuses on God's goodness in disposing all things for our benefit. In the same way, ingratitude breeds distrust, in that the ungrateful person already feels poorly cared for and has no reason to expect anything better in the future.

Third, complaint also reveals a worldly way of looking at things that ignores the deeper workings of providence. Rather than ask himself what God may intend by allowing a certain state of affairs (recalling how in the past he has often turned terrible misfortunes into wonderful blessings!), the complainer sees only the immediate inconveniences or irritations of his situation. He also fails to realize how fruitful this sacrifice may be.

Here I will allow myself to use rather strong language, with the excuse that I am directly quoting the apostle Paul. In his letter to the Philippians, Paul writes that "many live as enemies of the cross of Christ" (Phil. 3:18). He is referring explicitly to those whose "minds are set on earthly things" (v. 19). When we see discomfort as our greatest foe, we naturally flee from the cross, even when Christ intends it as a means of sanctification and fruitfulness for us.

You shouldn't conclude from these reflections that your only choice as a Christian is to "suck it up." A trusting, positive attitude doesn't blind us to the real hardships of life or the setbacks that we experience on a personal or an ecclesial level. Christ doesn't ask us to be Pollyannaish or stoic in our journey through this valley of tears. Moreover, as the great patriarchs and saints have demonstrated, God accepts our tears and entreaties with the greatest compassion. He empathizes with us and assists us in our need. What he does ask is that in our need we turn to him, not to another, and that we steadfastly confide in his love for us.

> Even though I walk through the darkest valley,
>   I fear no evil;
> for you are with me;
>   your rod and your staff—
>   they comfort me.

(Psalm 23:4)

DISCOURAGEMENT

Another enemy of trust is discouragement. Our lives often are no picnic, and a buildup of personal failures, unfair circumstances, and out-and-out misfortune can easily lead to dejection. While external adversity can often steel our resolve and impel us to further action, internal difficulties such as our moral failings and spiritual inconstancy often produce the opposite effect. How readily we lose enthusiasm in times of dryness or when we don't see much progress in our spiritual lives! How tempting to give up when we fall, especially when we fall repeatedly!

Yet the Lord invites us to confidence not *despite* our weakness, but *because* of it. Our poverty doesn't repel him; it moves his heart to compassion. He comes to the assistance of all who put their trust in him.

Nothing slows us down like discouragement. It saps our strength and enthusiasm and draws us deep into ourselves, shutting out the light and courage that the Holy Spirit gives.[2] Even when we have sunk very low, done very bad things, or have wandered away from God for a long time, hope is not only an option, it is an imperative. He always calls us back to himself, always desires our friendship, and always extends his mercy to anyone who needs it.

If we examine discouragement closely, we find some things that may surprise us. The first is that discouragement stems not from an excess of *humility*, but from an excess of *pride*. We often have such a high opinion of ourselves that when we don't perform to the standards we set for ourselves, we become disheartened. We exaggerate our own importance, as if our weakness and sins were somehow weightier than God's mercy and goodness.

Sometimes, too, discouragement appears because we don't know ourselves very well. We have an inflated idea of ourselves and of our own virtue, so when we fall we feel surprised, confused, and ashamed, and we want to give up. But here the pain comes not so much from having failed and offended *God*, but from wounded *self*-love. We are embarrassed and humiliated at seeing ourselves so weak.

Trust in God means shifting our focus from *our* littleness to *his* greatness. Discouragement normally appears when we stop looking at God (for whom all things are possible) and become fixated on ourselves and our own misery. It can even seem that discouragement is the "proper" or "humble" response to failure, as if a cheerful confidence in God somehow clashed with the reality of our own frailty.

In these situations it is especially helpful to treat discouragement as a *temptation*. Feeling sorry for ourselves and allowing discouragement to get a grip on us does no one any good. It doesn't help us, it doesn't please God, and it doesn't benefit other people. In fact, the only one who comes out ahead through our discouragement is the devil, who delights in seeing us doubt the love and mercy of God.

Think of good Peter, walking on the water, living in the midst of a miracle. The gospel says that "when he noticed how strong the wind was, he became afraid and started to sink" (Matt. 14:30 GOD'S WORD). In other words, as soon as he took his eyes off Christ and started looking about him, at the difficulties and at his own human inability to do what he was in fact doing, he began to sink. Our courage and confidence come from God's strength and fidelity, not our own. It is his power that raises us up and enables us to do many things that we could never do on our own.

We need the courage to get back up and start all over again with humility and confidence. God can bring wonderful things out of our failures and falls, beginning with a greater recognition of our weaknesses and our need for his grace. Discouragement, on the other hand, is a temptation the devil throws in our path to slow our spiritual progress and to make us waver in our commitment to Christ. Trust shows itself in a particularly beautiful way when we have fallen but still have the hope to grasp the hand of God, who reaches down to lift us up again.

SELF-SUFFICIENCY

One more important obstacle to trust is self-sufficiency. While self-sufficiency can go by many innocent-sounding names—*responsibility, autonomy, independence, self-reliance*—it always boils down to *pride*. And just as pride is the king of vices, so it is the greatest enemy of trust. As we become more and more inflated with our success, more confident in our own abilities, more sure of our own opinions, the less God seems like a needed savior and the more he seems like an intruder in our world. His commands become an unwanted imposition on our freedom and his offers of help an insulting attack on our ability to take care of ourselves.

It is humiliating to have to depend on someone else, and our natural tendency toward pride continuously tugs at us to assert ourselves and go it alone. Like a child that pulls his hand defiantly out of his mother's grasp in order to walk alone, we often seek to make our own way without God's help and without his rules.

All of this is a fiction, of course, and anyone who has read this far knows well that in and of ourselves, we can do nothing. But this knowledge does not stop pride from reappearing under a thousand guises. If we are to truly trust God, if we are to love him by trusting him, we need to learn to love our dependence on him. Rather than seeing this dependence as a mark of shame, we need to embrace it as a liberating truth of the human condition.

Trust is based on the intimate conviction that we cannot do it alone, and thus humility is a prerequisite for trust. Acknowledging our neediness and poverty, our need of a redeemer, sets us up to ask for and expect the assistance that Christ offers. Not one of us is his or her own savior, even though we would often like to be. We need humility to recognize our weaknesses. We need humility in order to ask for God's help. We need humility to relinquish the steering wheels of our lives and allow the Holy Spirit to drive.

A soul that abases itself is all-powerful before God. It is our littleness and our nothingness that he responds to. We sometimes think we need to impress God and win him over by showing him what wonderful things we are capable of. Like the Pharisee, we pull out our list of qualities and accomplishments as if we were expecting God to step back and say, "Wow! You are one impressive Christian! Now I know why I love you so much!" That isn't going to happen. As in the case of the Pharisee, such self-aggrandizement merely makes God shake his head sadly, wondering when we are going to get over our infatuation with ourselves and allow him into our hearts.

Humility and trust are sisters. They naturally go together and complete each other. Humility without trust easily slides into discouragement, while trust without humility quickly morphs into vain presumption. When we are able to practice both these virtues together, we become deeply aware that without God's grace, we are nothing and can do nothing, but we become equally aware that with him there is nothing we cannot do. Our self-reliance turns into God-reliance.

YOU MAY TRUST MORE THAN YOU REALIZE

After slogging through these sins against trust, you might be about ready to throw in the towel. We can easily get down on ourselves, since we all recognize traces of these sins in our own lives. But don't be too quick to give up. The fact is that you probably trust God a good deal more than you even realize.

Do you pray? I don't think you would do that if you didn't trust God to hear and answer you. You might do it once or twice, in the vain hope that "someone" was out there, but you wouldn't do it with any regularity. A regular prayer life is a sure sign that you trust God. Sure, your prayer life could be better—more intimate, more conversational, less self-centered— but the fact that you pray means you've already got an important piece in place.

Do you try to live according to God's will? I doubt very much that you would do that if you didn't trust in God. You believe in him. You believe he has a will for you. You believe that one day you will be judged by him. All of these things mean that you believe in his word and trust in his promises. Why else would you bother? Could your efforts be better and more constant? Undoubtedly. Yet your desire to please him and to improve is already a sign that you trust in him and love him.

Where do you turn in your hour of need? You probably know, deep down, that in many of life's toughest circumstances, God alone can help you. You trust in your family and friends, but ultimately you trust in God to save you. He alone holds the key to your existence and awaits you in eternity. Like fearful Peter walking across the water with unsteady sea legs, you tremble and sometimes falter, but when you do, you throw yourself on Jesus and cry out to him: "Lord, save me!"

Could you trust more? Sure you could. But this doesn't mean your trust is not real. Take courage!

So trust in God is one way of showing God that we love him. It is a gift we give him. Unfortunately, it's easier to see the value of trust than it is to actually trust. Even if we choose to trust, we run up against real obstacles. Let's look at some of these so we can better overcome them.

WHY TRUSTING IS SO HORRIBLY HARD

8

WHY DO WE HAVE TROUBLE TRUSTING?

In his teaching, Jesus says many tough things. He says that it is harder for a rich man to enter the kingdom of heaven than for a camel to pass through the eye of a needle (see Matt. 19:24). He talks about taking up one's cross every day (see Luke 9:23) in order to follow him. He speaks of the difficulty of accepting his teaching regarding marriage and divorce (see Matt. 19:11), and his disciples complain about how hard it is to accept his discourse on the bread of life (see John 6:60). But of all the truly tough things that Jesus asks of his followers, I wonder if there is any as tough as unconditional trust. Sure, self-denial is hard. Sure, obeying the commandments is hard. But trust is harder.

Why is it so difficult to trust in God? We have already looked at some reasons. Our natural desire for security drives us to look for sure things and to avoid the risk that trust entails. We are more rationalistic today than people were in former times, too, and this makes us wary of believing

For me, there's nothing harder than trust. I don't know why but I just can't seem to do it. I would almost rather that God ask me for anything else than to trust him absolutely. I wish he would show me things rather than [ask me to] believe what I can't see. I mean, how can you do that in this day and age?

—JAMIE, AGE 32

anything we can't empirically verify. Also, our contact with many other cultures and belief systems can throw our certainties for a loop, since we realize that many people think differently than we do. Perhaps the biggest factor that separates our age from past times, however, is our experience of *betrayal*. Betrayal has always been around, of course, but never to the degree that it is today. Our contemporary society permits irresponsibility like no other society before it. It is easy to get out of marriage when things become uncomfortable; it is easy to dodge commitments when they start to weigh on us, and our culture encourages us to do so. Unfortunately, when one person ducks out of his responsibility, someone else suffers the consequences. We all have been on the receiving end of this unfaithfulness, and it isn't pleasant.

In this chapter I would like to explore with you some other elements that make trust difficult for today's Christians. The better we know the causes of our distrust, the more easily we can confront and hopefully overcome them. Let's look first of all at how our temperament can influence our ability to trust God.

TRUST AND TEMPERAMENT

We all know people who find it quite natural to trust, and others for whom trusting is like pulling teeth. Sometimes the differences can be due to people's experiences, but there are other factors as well, including our inborn dispositions. Some people are naturally more optimistic and see the sunny side of everything. Even after being let down, they bounce back with relative ease. Others seem skeptical by nature and are inclined to see the dark side of every situation. Some people, too, find it hard to trust because of the risk it entails. Psychologists also describe people as "risk-averse" or "risk-tolerant," depending on their natural willingness to gamble, with other variants such as "risk-neutral" and "risk-loving" (or risk-seeking). These factors have a lot to do with trust, since trust always entails risk.

These habitual ways of being are aspects of *temperament*, the personality one is born with. Temperament refers to the ensemble of a person's natural disposition, aptitudes, and inclinations, or the genetic component of personality. No one's choices are predetermined by temperament (we are free, after all), but temperament does influence the way we see and experience things. So the same situation may provoke very different reactions in people of different temperament.

There are several systems for describing temperament. The ancient Greeks spoke of four temperaments—choleric, sanguine, melancholic, and phlegmatic—which they believed derived from the predominance of a given fluid (or "humor") in a person's body (yellow bile, black bile, blood, or phlegm). Newer, more complex systems for describing temperament break down the fundamental components of temperament and then recombine them into temperament types. René Le Senne, for instance, delineated three fundamental categories, which he called activity (active/ passive), resonance (primary/secondary), and emotivity (emotive/non-emotive). The combinations of these possibilities yield a series of eight possible temperaments.

You have probably also heard of Meyer Friedman's simpler description of type A personalities (aggressive, driven, industrious) and type B personalities (agreeable, laid-back, easygoing), or the Jungian archetypes. All of these systems attempt, in a more or less successful way, to describe the natural base of qualities that predispose us to behave in a given way. The point here is not to explain or compare these models, but simply to examine how temperament (or personality type) affects our ability to trust in God.

For simplicity's sake, let's look for a moment at the four ancient temperaments. According to this system, the *choleric* person—a natural leader—would have particular trouble trusting, because he (or she) is often convinced that he can do a better job than others. He is assertive and likes to take matters in hand, and he gets impatient when he has to wait for others to do things. *If you want something done right, do it yourself.* This self-reliance easily extends even to one's relationship with God, where trust can feel like a flimsy support compared with the self-assurance of one's own abilities and strengths.

To grow in trust, a choleric person needs to exercise profound humility before God and others, learning to accept his own weaknesses and needs. Patience, too, is a quality that a choleric person must acquire in order to be able to accept God's timetable instead of imposing his own.

A *sanguine* person, on the other hand, may find trust more natural but lack the depth needed to continue steadfast in spite of difficulties. By nature, a sanguine person is easygoing, friendly, and changeable, with frequent mood shifts and ups and downs. He or she may trust in one moment, then abandon all hope in the next. Unless this fickleness is brought under control, the sanguine person may never achieve a stable trust that would ground his life for the long haul.

A *melancholic* person enjoys greater depth and stability than a sanguine but tends to see things from the negative side. Once betrayed, the melancholic finds it incredibly difficult to trust again. Melancholics also tend to be more suspicious and reserved than people of other temperaments, and they are not quick to place their trust in anyone else. They do not naturally expect the best, and this pessimism can be reflected in their relationship with God as well. They need to cultivate a healthy optimism and to contemplate the goodness and steadfastness of God.

The *phlegmatic* temperament is characterized by inactivity and calm, with tranquillity being a value held in high regard. While not particularly untrusting of others, a phlegmatic person tends to be risk-averse, since such dependence on others (especially others who ask things of him) becomes a burden and a threat to his personal peace and well-being. More than the other temperaments, people of phlegmatic temperament need to confront the challenges of trusting in others and take courage to expose themselves to the risk this entails.

While in no way comprehensive, this brief look at the role of temperament in trusting illustrates how different people need to approach trust in different ways. What comes easily to one person may be exceedingly difficult for another. Growing in trust means knowing ourselves as well. Depending on our personality type, our trust issues will vary, as will the remedies we need to apply to trust more and better.

MORAL OBSTACLES TO TRUST

Along with the innate, temperamental components that make trust easier or harder, there are other factors that can influence our ability to trust. Some of these are moral, related to our good and bad choices, the formation of our consciences, and our moral frailty. If we are to grow in trust, we need to capitalize on the positive aspects and minimize the negative. Recognizing the elements at play, as listed below, may better equip us to deal with those possible obstacles.

DELICACY OF CONSCIENCE

A first obstacle to trust on the moral level could be your *delicacy of conscience*. Whereas this moral sensitivity is a very good thing—a gift, really—it can also run amok if not coupled with a deep confidence in God's love. If you possess a delicate conscience, you are probably acutely aware of your sinfulness and failings. You know how unworthy you are of God's mercy and grace and that you deserve nothing from him. But perhaps you focus more on your personal misery than on God's goodness. Delicacy of conscience sometimes slips into extreme scrupulosity. *Why should God be good to me?* we rightly wonder. *It would serve me right for God to abandon me forever, since that is what I deserve.*

Here a good rule of thumb is that *nothing* should be allowed to jeopardize your confidence in God. Nothing at all, least of all your unworthiness. God is infinitely better and more merciful than you think he is. Remember, too, that your trust in Christ is a gift *you* give *him*, and that distrust wounds his heart even more than your other imperfections. When you trust in him absolutely, you fill him with delight. So use your desire for perfection to grow in the virtue that pleases Christ most: your confidence in him.

Where delicacy of conscience represents one end of the spectrum, the other end presents its own obstacles to trust. Allow me to highlight two of these.

OUR UNWORTHINESS OF TRUST

First, sometimes our own unworthiness of trust leads us to doubt others, even God. It is rightly said that people's judgment of others often says more about themselves than about the one judged. We tend to project our own goodness or badness onto others, and a person who is unfaithful expects others to be unfaithful as well. Distrust—like trust—reveals as much about the person distrusting as the one distrusted.

If a thief sees a man putting a ladder up against the side of a house, he readily suspects that the man is attempting to break in and rob the house—because that is what the thief would do! We attribute to others the motives and intentions that fill our own hearts. There is a famous story told about three men who all witness the same scene but come up with wildly different interpretations of what is going on.

The basic facts of the matter are these: A man is seen walking up to the door of a house at 4:00 p.m. A woman opens the door and admits him. Meanwhile, three other people drive by during this short interlude and see the man enter the house. All see the exact same thing happen, but each imagines something different. One fellow, a good and honest man himself, thinks: *How nice! That man has come home from work early to spend extra time with his wife and family.* The second witness thinks, *Hmmm, I bet that man came home from work early to check up on his wife and see what she is up to.* The third man witnesses the scene and thinks, *Oho, that is a lover coming in for a little tryst before the husband gets home.*

Here the curious thing is that the facts of the matter don't change; only the interpretation does. Furthermore, it isn't that the three witnesses see different elements that make them more or less suspicious of what is going on. Rather, each projects onto the man's intentions something that he carries inside.

Even though God doesn't deserve it, he isn't exempt from our self-projection. If we are noble and generous, we spontaneously assume that God behaves in a

> *Once you've been around for a while you realize how foolish it is to trust others. I don't really trust anyone anymore. And frankly, I think people are stupid to trust me. That's not cynicism; it's realism.*
>
> —AARON, AGE 47

similar way. If we are petty, we easily think of God as petty. So what happens when we are unfaithful, unworthy of other people's confidence? We can project this same untrustworthiness onto God. Here we would do well to meditate on the apostle Paul's words, which we looked at earlier: "If we are faithless, he remains faithful—for he cannot deny himself" (2 Tim. 2:13). God's faithfulness does not depend on our own.

Perhaps we are not morally bad and unfaithful, but just lazy and somewhat indifferent. In this case as well, we may bring God down to our own level and expect indifference from him. We may doubt the passion of God's commitment to us, especially if we have never experienced the depths of his love. We may think that God is as indifferent to us as we are to him. *God has so many other, more important things to worry about,* we may think, *and better people to dedicate himself to. Why should he care about me? I can't be very high on his list of priorities.*

If you are tempted to think this way, more meditation on God's infinite goodness is in order. Look at Jesus on the cross. Ask yourself (better yet, ask him!) why he is there. He will no doubt respond that he is there for you, because he loves you. Not for "humanity" in some abstract sense, but *you.* He is there to save you from your sins and your pettiness, and he is also there to demonstrate the extremes to which his love will go for you. His suffering shouts out to you: "This is how much I love you! Believe in my love!" He will not easily let you go.

PRIDE

A more hard-core moral obstacle comes in the shape of our pride. We have already seen that some can see trust in God and his mercy as just a cop-out. Thinking they are taking the moral high road, such people may think: *I don't deserve it, so I shouldn't even look for it. I deserve whatever punishment is coming to me.* Though such people think they are being tough and brutally honest, in reality they are letting themselves be deceived by the father of lies. Behind that half-truth ("I deserve whatever is coming to me") stands the far more important truth that God does not will that for me. He wills my union with him forever in heaven. He wants me to be saved! He already took upon himself what I deserve and paid my ransom. We each need the humility and gratitude to accept that free gift. That is the truly noble way. That is the high road.

By its very nature grace is freely given. It cannot be earned. Trust is hard because it makes us vulnerable, dependent, limited. Better said, trust doesn't *make* us vulnerable, since we already *are* vulnerable. Trust forces us to *acknowledge* our dependence and vulnerability. We realize that we are debtors, that we are not self-made men and women. We didn't earn it. We didn't pay our way. Jesus did.

WHEN TRUST GETS ESPECIALLY TOUGH

These are some general considerations of how our moral state can affect our ability and willingness to trust in God. But sometimes we face particular situations that make trust in God much harder than usual. Let's look at a few samples of these.

WHEN MR. (OR MRS.) RIGHT NEVER COMES ALONG

Christians generally believe that God intends them to marry specific people. When those persons don't show up, we can begin to doubt God's fidelity. Let me describe one such case, which speaks for many more.

Linda is an intelligent, attractive, and genuinely good person. She is a committed Christian and a well-rounded individual who would make a fine catch for anyone. In spite of this, she has never found "the right man." Linda dated only occasionally during her twenties, because she assumed that God would let her know when the right man came along and was in no rush to secure a husband. So she dedicated herself to her studies and her career, making time for important apostolic works.

As she approached thirty, however, Linda began to become concerned that no stable relationship seemed forthcoming. The situation only worsened between the ages of thirty and thirty-five, since Linda realized her desire for home and family was growing and, as she said to me, her "biological clock was ticking away."

As the months and years went by, Linda began to question God's plan for her. What had gone wrong? Why had God treated her like this when she had always tried to live according to his will? Little by little, she began to be overwhelmed by the feeling that God had failed her. She had trusted, and God had not come through for her.

Then questions came pouring in. Since God couldn't be at fault, it must be her, Linda thought. *Where did I go wrong? Did I miss some sign along the way? Should I have taken so-and-so more seriously, rather than wait for someone better? Is this God's way of telling me that I missed the boat altogether? That I should have gone into the convent or consecrated life?* These and many more doubts plagued her prayers and quiet times, leading her to distress and inner turmoil.

This situation led to a profound trial of Linda's trust in God. Everything that earlier had appeared so clear and straightforward now seemed jumbled and topsy-turvy. Her former securities seemed so distant and so . . . false. Had it all been a dream? Had she been naive to think that God would show her the way?

As extreme as this case may seem, it is really quite typical. Many people who try to follow Christ closely run into just this sort of wall at some point in their lives. Sometimes it resolves itself quickly, and the person returns to a state of relative peace and equilibrium. Other times it lasts for months, even years. Still other times—sadly—it results in a permanent loss of faith and trust in God as a loving and providing Father.

Thankfully, in Linda's case the story ended well. She suffered, to be sure. But in the end she recovered her serenity, accepting the fact that she would probably never marry, but that God had other important and exciting plans for her life. She trusts him as much as ever.

WHEN A MARRIED COUPLE ISN'T ABLE TO CONCEIVE A CHILD

Another frequent occurrence that deeply tries Christians' trust in God is the failure to conceive a child. Though I have known many couples who have experienced this ordeal, I will describe one in greater detail, allowing them to speak for the rest. Ed and Karen were a fairly typical Christian couple—enthusiastic, God-fearing, and anxious to live out their married vocation united to the Lord. This sort of couple is a pastor's delight. They are virtuous and pure, open to God's plan, looking forward to raising their children as future citizens of heaven. One need only encourage them to keep moving forward, steadfast in their good intentions.

The marriage was a beautiful, holy affair. Both Ed and Karen had prepared well for this special day, meditating on the meaning of the marriage covenant and getting their spiritual lives fully in order for this momentous sacrament. They didn't take their commitment lightly but understood what it meant to commit themselves to each other for life, before God and in the presence of the Christian community. With great personal sacrifice, they had refrained from sexual activity before marriage, determined as they were to follow God's law in everything. And now the great day had arrived when they could give themselves to each other fully and completely, sure of his blessing and his companionship.

The first months of marriage were lived in earthly bliss. Ed commented to me that he had never thought he could be so happy. Sure they had their little tiffs, he said, but they always made up, and nothing wounded their union in a serious way. Wanting to make their marriage a truly godly enterprise, they prayed together each day, making sure God's will was at the center of their intentions and priorities. They went to work each morning excited at the prospect that at the end of the day they would be together once more, living out their vocation in all its beauty and intimacy.

It was seven months before the first dark cloud appeared on the horizon. The first indication I had was a chance meeting with Karen. She seemed abnormally preoccupied, and even her attempts to smile and wish me a pleasant day couldn't hide her underlying concern. I asked her if something was wrong and she insisted that there wasn't, but after a minute or so she opened up, saying, "It has been seven months and we still haven't conceived." I assured her that it often takes couples a while to get pregnant and invited her to renew her trust in God. "He knows what he is doing," I said in earnest. "I know he does," she agreed with a broad smile of relief.

But two more months went by and still nothing had happened. Karen returned to me, much more worried than on the previous occasion. "Is that all I should do?" she blurted out. "Just keep waiting for God to do something?" "Well, you have to do your part," I replied, smiling, trying to lighten the air a bit. "I know," she said seriously, looking down and shaking her head. "That isn't it. I don't know where the problem is, with him or with me." We prayed an "Our Father" together and entrusted their marriage and future family to God's paternal care. The conversation changed to other things, and soon Karen was all smiles again, lighthearted and full of confidence. She said good-bye and drove off.

It wasn't long before I received a phone call from Ed, asking for an appointment so the three of us could speak together. We agreed to meet the following Wednesday, and soon the time for the meeting arrived. The three of us sat for a moment in silence, they on the couch and I in an armchair, and then Ed broke the ice. "We want to go have some tests done—," he began.

Karen interrupted, "That wouldn't mean a lack of trust in God, would it?"

"No, of course not," I said. "Use all the moral means at your disposal to figure out what God wants from you. There's nothing wrong with having a doctor help you understand what is going on with you." I knew that they would do nothing to compromise their marriage commitments or offend their marital chastity.

The tests came back two weeks later, showing no abnormalities. As much as this seemed like good news, it only added to the anguish. Sometimes it helps to know where the problem lies, since it allows us to focus somewhere, and sometimes to look for a solution. Six more months went by without our having much contact. Both Ed and Karen were working on pressing projects at work, and this seemed to alleviate the stress of their situation, at least for the time being. I, too, had plenty of other things going on, but still prayed daily for God to make himself present in their lives and to grant them the gift of a child. "After all," I prayed, "so many people reject their children or even get pregnant without wanting to. Here you have a couple who desperately want to have a child. Don't you think it would be a good idea to let them get pregnant?"

Out of the blue Ed showed up at my door one day, asking to talk. He explained to me that their marriage had become laced with tension. Usually easygoing, Karen had grown more and more irritable and would suddenly turn on him, apparently for no reason. At least that was the way Ed saw things, though he admitted that he was more uptight than usual, too. "I just don't know what God wants anymore," he said. "Things used to seem so clear, and now nothing is. I feel like he has abandoned us."

I suggested that the couple go on a marriage-renewal retreat, to try to sort things out better before the Lord. I reminded him of how many other people suffer similar things, and that God always has a plan and always is faithful, though we may not see it until later on. We set a tentative date for the retreat, and he left to propose the idea to Karen.

To make a long story short, Ed and Karen slowly became reconciled to the idea that perhaps God had other plans for them and accepted the fact that they might never have children. They started to seek other ways to serve and devoted several hours each week as volunteers working with handicapped children.

Another year and a half went by, when one day I received a phone call from Ed. "You won't believe this, Padre," he said. "We're pregnant!" Ed broke down and cried for a while before he could speak again. "God is so good," he finally said. "I'm so sorry I doubted him."

Many times the story doesn't end like this, of course. Many couples can never have children. Some adopt. Others find alternative ways to fill their lives as a couple. But all of them suffer. And all of them find their trust in God strained, or at least put to the test.

WHEN WE FALL INTO A MORAL RUT AND CAN'T GET OUT

Another situation that can put a Christian's trust to the test is the painful experience of falling into a habitual pattern of sin and vice. Sin always involves personal choice, of course. It is something we freely commit, rather than something that happens *to us*. But it is also true that sin can become a habit, where it becomes increasingly difficult to push the urge to sin aside. I have known countless men and women who fall into one sin or another and, despite their goodwill and sincere repentance, seem unable to climb out of the hole in which sin has trapped them. They can start to feel truly helpless, and more and more unworthy of God's forgiveness and help. When people find themselves in this situation, their trust in God often begins to waver.

For some, it may be the habit of gossip or criticism even of friends behind their backs. In spite of a genuine desire to change, this habit can become so rooted that people feel unable to change for long. As soon as they let their guard down, they find themselves once again speaking ill of others or making known their faults and foibles.

For others, it may be impatience with a loved one, such as a spouse. Many times the people we live with take the brunt of our pettiness, and even when we want to treat them well, this good proposal might not last for long. We may be patient for a while, but then those little quirks that we find so irritating get the upper hand, and we find ourselves upset again.

For others, it may be a habit of sexual sin, such as the use of pornography or masturbation. This can create a dependency or addiction and cause a deep sense of angst and frustration. Our relationships with others can be undermined as well. Wives can feel betrayed by their husbands who commit these sexual sins, and a sense of inadequacy and shame creates a wall between the spouses. The omnipresence of sexual stimulation, especially through the Internet, has been a source of suffering for countless individuals and couples, and these types of habits often seem particularly hard to break.

The list goes on and on. Sin, especially when it is habitual, can create a sense of powerlessness. We lose self-dominion and the experience of being in control of our own lives. Worse still, it seems that even when we pray, God does not help us to overcome the vices that tie us down. When a situation like this lasts for months, even years, our confidence in God can be severely tested. Here we cannot help but think of the apostle Paul and his own experience with the heavy hand of sin:

> I find it to be a law that when I want to do what is good, evil lies close at hand. For I delight in the law of God in my inmost self, but I see in my members another law at war with the law of my mind, making me captive to the law of sin that dwells in my members. Wretched man that I am! Who will rescue me from this body of death? Thanks be to God through Jesus Christ our Lord! So then, with my mind I am a slave to the law of God, but with my flesh I am a slave to the law of sin. (Romans 7:21–25)

Here, true trust in God keeps us fighting, knowing that his grace is stronger than our sin. His power manifests itself most dramatically when we are weak. And so we refuse to throw in the towel. We refuse to accept Satan's lies that sin and death will triumph. We refuse to give sin the final word in our lives, since we have a Savior who loves us and shed his blood for us. We know that he intends that we be saints, "holy and blameless before him in love" (Eph. 1:4).

And where will we find the strength to keep fighting and eventually to conquer sin in our lives? Only in him. As Christ promised Paul, "My grace is sufficient for you, for power is made perfect in weakness" (2 Cor. 12:9).

Obviously, these few examples show just the tip of the iceberg. Each one of us could draw up a list of times and situations that have been particularly difficult for our trust in God. Recognizing that others struggle, too, can help us take courage to face our own difficulties in this area. I write these things as much for myself as I do for you, since trust is something that I constantly must grapple with.

Surely the hardest hurdle to overcome is the experience of feeling let down by God. Natural problems, even sufferings and sorrows, can be borne as long as we feel that God is at our side, strengthening and consoling us. But what about when God seems to leave us? Let's look more closely at this trying experience and what we can learn from it.

9

WHAT TO DO WHEN
GOD LETS YOU DOWN

Human beings can bear a lot. We can bear getting sick. We can bear it when an employee or business partner cheats on us. We can bear it when a child gets punished at school for fighting with another kid. Though it hurts, we can accept human frailty, knowing we all are made of the same clay. We may not like it, but we understand that it happens. What is not so understandable is when God lets us down.

Disappointment in God must be one of the saddest experiences of the spiritual life. God is our Father. He made us and we belong to him. He is the one who should never let us down. Yet it is not uncommon for Christians to feel God has abandoned them and left them in the dark. They placed all their hope in him, and in the end they feel he has betrayed them.

You surely remember the scene after Christ's resurrection when two of his former disciples are trudging sadly away from Jerusalem toward the town of Emmaus, convinced that their hopes in Jesus have proved groundless (see Luke 24:13–35). He persuaded them to leave everything to follow him, and they believed in him. They trusted him when he said he was the Messiah. And now they feel they have been made to look like fools. Their family members and friends had been right, after all, when they warned them not to take up with "that itinerant preacher man." They had said he was probably a fraud. They had said the two disciples would live to regret it, and now they did.

And as they walk along their way, feeling disheartened and betrayed, Jesus himself comes and begins to walk with them. Not recognizing him, they try to explain to him about Jesus, how he performed great works, and how in the end the chief priests and leaders handed him over to death. And then they reveal their own disillusion, with some of the saddest words in Scripture. "We had hoped that he was the one to redeem Israel" (Luke 24:21). "We had hoped. . . ." *No, we no longer hope. We no longer believe. He let us down. We had believed, hoped, given up everything, and now we have to return empty-handed, feeling like dolts for having trusted him.*

Yet Jesus himself, the Good Shepherd, comes to the rescue. He seeks them out and leads them back to the fold. He reveals to them the deeper truth about his own suffering and death, and little by little their hope returns. Their hearts begin to burn within them as the flame of trust is re-kindled. In the end, they recognize him as he breaks bread for them. They rush back to Jerusalem to give the good news to the other disciples.

WHO TURNED OFF THE LIGHTS?

We can identify with the experience of these two disciples. One of the diffi-culties in the spiritual life is an experience of God's absence or silence. People who seriously pursue holiness often share a common experience. From one day to the next, an intimate, personal, trusting relationship with God seems to become dry, dark, cold, and utterly distant. Who turned off the lights?

In the course of my interviews with people for this book, again and again I heard a similar response. One of the hardest things about trusting God is the experience of abandonment. Some used the term "darkness," others "silence," others "absence." But in the end, they were describing a similar experience. *Where did God go? Why did he leave? Did I do something wrong?* It is relatively easy to keep trusting as long as the other person is close. But things change when the person is far away.

One of the most revered figures of the past century was a small, unas-suming Albanian nun by the name of Mother Teresa of Calcutta. People around the world admired her because of her tireless dedication to the poorest of the poor. She went where no one else would go, loving the un-loved, caring for those who had no one. Teresa attended to those living in the shadows and dark corners of life—the poor, the dying, the abandoned, the unwanted. That figure captured the world's imagination. Yet Teresa always spoke of the deeper poverty of the spirit—the poverty that comes from not knowing God and living far from him.

Teresa had little confidence in political programs to eliminate poverty. She simply dedicated herself to the people she encountered, cleansing their wounds, holding their frail bodies, and offering them the smile of Christ. She did so taking Jesus' words at face value: *Whatever you do to the least of these, you do to me* (see Matt. 25:40).

Because of the characteristic broad smile across her lined face and her unflagging determination in serving the poor, people assumed that Teresa enjoyed a lively, intimate interior life with Jesus, adorned with consolations and spiritual warmth. *She gives up a lot,* people assumed, *but at least she has the close company of God in her soul.* In 2007 some startling revelations shattered this common belief. It turns out that for nearly fifty years Teresa struggled with dense interior darkness. The exhaustive review of Teresa's written correspondence for her beatification process unveiled a woman few knew, a woman who loved Jesus to the point of suffering for him and sharing in his abandonment. She strode doggedly forward in her appointed mission, but without feeling God's presence. She walked in faith amid blackness and trusted in God with no interior consolations.

A book of her journal and letters, edited by Father Brian Kolodiejchuk, was released in late 2007 under the title *Come Be My Light.* "If I ever become a saint, I will surely be one of 'darkness,'" she wrote. "I will continually be absent from heaven—to light the light of those in darkness on Earth."[1]

We usually assume that as we draw closer to God we will experience feelings of peace, serenity, and interior joy. In fact, for those beginning the spiritual life, this is frequently the case. God often grants these consolations so we might not tire in our spiritual pursuits. But from the writings of many great friends of God we know that sometimes, for those more advanced in the spiritual life, God withholds those consolations. He does so to purify his followers so that they may seek him only for his own sake, and not for the good feelings that may bring. Saint John of the Cross called this purifying experience the "dark night of the soul," during which the soul feels as if someone has turned out the lights on the spiritual life. Like so many other aspects of the spiritual life, this one finds a point of reference in Jesus' own life.

> You know what's funny? I trusted God. I really did. In the end he pushed me away. I kept trusting, and he kept punishing me for it. I would rely on him for something, and he would systematically let me down. He was so hard on me I couldn't take it anymore, and in the end I said, "That's enough!" I cannot understand how a good God would treat his children this way. I used to trust God when I was younger. I really did. But he pushed me away.
>
> —SAMANTHA, AGE 40

Throughout his life Jesus exhibited absolute confidence in his Father. He knew that the Father was with him, that he always heard him. He walked at ease with God, a Son with his Father. Yet things got mighty tough for him, too, and his trust was tried, perhaps even more than ours is. In the Garden of Gethsemane his soul was "overwhelmed with sorrow to the point of death" (Mark 14:34 NIV). The next day, Jesus experienced such loneliness on the cross that he cried out "My God, my God, why have you abandoned me?" (Mark 15:34 GOD'S WORD). It was not only the adoring crowds who had left him alone, not only his chosen disciples who had all run away; now it appeared that even his Father was nowhere to be found. And yet even here we find Jesus trusting, confident in his Father's love. "Father, into your hands I entrust my spirit" (Luke 23:46 GOD'S WORD).

WHAT IS GOD UP TO?

Why does God permit this? Why does he treat his friends this way? It is often difficult, so as not to say impossible, to understand why God does what he does, or even what he is doing with us at any given moment. Often we are left completely in the dark and must cling to our trust that he knows what he is doing. Our faith assures us that our experiences are ultimately for our good. He allows things only out of love for us, even when it isn't apparent. A story is told that clearly illustrates this idea. It is a simple story, nothing more than a children's tale really, but perhaps it will say something to you.

There was an elderly couple in London who liked to visit the small handicraft shops near the city center. On entering one of these, the couple was struck by the beauty of one small teacup, placed with care atop one of the display counters. The woman took the cup in her hands, admiring its beauty and the detail of its craftsmanship. "I have never seen anything so fine!" she exclaimed to her husband.

In the hands of the woman, the teacup began to speak. "May I tell you a little of my story?" the cup began, "because I was not always as you see me now.

"A long time ago I was just a lump of clay. One day, a craftsman picked me up and began to work me between his fingers. He placed me on a table and hammered me with his palms until I had to cry out. He began to mold me into a shape, stretching me and pinching me. I begged him to leave me alone, and he would not. 'Please, you are hurting me,' I pleaded. 'I am happy the way I am. Just leave me in peace.' But the crafts-man said to me, 'I am not finished with you yet. Hold on a little longer.'

"Next the craftsman placed me in a terribly hot oven. I had never felt such tremendous heat. I beat against the little window of the oven and through it I could see the craftsman mouthing the words, 'I am not finished with you yet. Hold on a little longer.'

"When at last he opened the oven door the craftsman put me on a shelf where I slowly began to cool and recover some calm. Yet I had barely cooled when he picked me up once again and began to scrape me and sand me with rough paper, until I felt that my very skin was coming off. I shouted for him to stop, but he continued mercilessly. He would stop and look at me from time to time, squinting and turn-ing me around in his hand. He seemed oblivious to my supplications.

"Next the craftsman pulled out several small jars and a few fine brushes and began to apply paint to me. I felt that I was suffocating as he meticulously spread paint over every inch of me. Again I shouted out for him to stop and again he gently said to me, 'I am not finished with you yet. Hold on a little longer.'

"Finally, when I thought he had finished with his tortures, the craftsman unexpectedly placed me in yet another oven, even hotter than the first. The heat of the kiln was so intense that I was sure my life was over. I wept and cried out at the top of my lungs, but the craftsman didn't seem to care. I begged him to respect me, to take me out, to leave me alone, but all in vain. He only repeated the same words: 'I am not finished with you yet. Hold on a little longer.'

"I don't know how I survived the whole cruel treatment. Somehow I held on and was able to get through every new torture that the crafts-man subjected me to. At last, the craftsman opened the door and took me lovingly in his hands and carried me to a very different place. It was absolutely beautiful. Around me I saw cups and vases of the most varied sorts, one more stunning than the other. They were true works of art, something I had seen only in my dreams.

"Not much time had passed when I realized that I was in a shop, and before me was a looking glass. When I first peered into it I thought it was a window, and the figure before my eyes another of the works that surrounded me. I could not believe *I* was that beautiful teacup I was contemplating in the mirror. That couldn't be me!

"Then my craftsman approached and said to me, 'I know that you suf-fered when I molded you with my hands, but look now at your beautiful figure. I know that you endured terrible heat in my kilns, but observe your solidity and integrity. I know that the scraping and polishing hurt like nothing else you had experienced, but now look at the evenness of your texture. And the paint made you feel sick, but now consider the beauty of your color and the radiance of your shine. Imagine if I had left you the way I found you! Now, at last, you are a finished work. You are exactly what I pictured when I began to work on you. You are beloved to me.'"

I am sure you understand the message of this simple story. Paul com-pares us to clay pots, formed in God's hands (see Rom. 9:20–21). Only God knows what he is making out of each of us. Only he understands the point and purpose of each stage of this process. Perhaps we can identify with the teacup. Perhaps we find ourselves being rubbed and scraped or suffering the heat of the kiln. Perhaps we cry out to God because we do not understand, and he acts as if he doesn't hear us, or doesn't care. I am convinced this is not the case. I am also convinced that one day the meaning of each moment, of each little suffering, will be brought to light. And we will be beautiful.

> *Ther...*
> *God ...*
> *though ...*
> *stop n...*
> *change ...*
> *back I* realize *I felt a sense of anger toward God. Yet I now see they were blessings and have made me the person I am today.*
>
> —ALEX, AGE 25

GOD'S PEDAGOGY

The apostle Paul speaks about milk and solid food. Milk is for infants who cannot yet chew, while solid food is for bigger children and adults who are ready for more. God weans us off milk so we can consume more substantive fare. This is true in our life of trust as well. He wants us to move beyond an innocent, untried trust to a mature trust that has stood the test of time and trials. Paul wrote: "Brothers and sisters, I could not speak to you as spiritual people, but rather as people of the flesh, as infants in Christ. I fed you with milk, not solid food, for you were not ready for solid food. Even now you are still not ready, for you are still of the flesh" (1 Cor. 3:1–3).

What does "milk" refer to in our spiritual lives? Little children need constant encouragement. They need to be led by the hand, and sometimes even carried. They haven't yet acquired the necessary mettle to forge onward despite difficulties. Like little children, people "of the flesh" depend on consolations and spiritual gifts in order to stay faithful to God and trust in his love. As people grow into spiritual adulthood, however, they learn more and more to love God for his own sake rather than for the gifts stows on them. The little consolations become less necessary, they are ready for solid food.

When God begins to put our trust to the test, then, it is not a bad sign but a good one. It means that God thinks we are ready for more. He thinks it's time to put us on a more nutritious, grown-up diet of solid food.

The Bible uses another analogy to describe the way God purifies us. It compares God's purification to the work of a goldsmith or silversmith who purifies precious metals to make them still more beautiful and valuable. In the book of Proverbs we read: "The crucible is for silver, and the furnace is for gold, but the LORD tests the heart" (17:3). Both the crucible and the furnace are unpleasant prospects. No one wants to be heated to a very high temperature in order to burn off impurities, but this is how gold and silver are made pure. There is no other way. The book of Wisdom offers a more prolonged explanation of the meaning of this purification:

> If before men, indeed, they be punished, yet is their hope full of immortality; chastised a little, they shall be greatly blessed, because God tried them and found them worthy of himself. As gold in the furnace, he proved them, and as sacrificial offerings he took them to himself. In the time of their visitation they shall shine, and shall dart about as sparks through stubble. (Wisdom 3:4–7 NAB)

The saints who wrote about their experiences of a dark night agree that it is a purifying experience. As gold is tested in the fire, God often purifies those who love him by detaching them from other things, especially from themselves. He does this not so we will lose trust in him, but so we learn to live by a deeper, more resilient faith.

One of the hardest things to understand about God's action in our lives (or perhaps I should say his apparent inaction) is his *timing*. We wonder why he seems so slow at times to register our needs and act on them. At other times he acts in the least opportune moment, rather than when we are prepared and well disposed. What is going on here, and what does it have to do with our trust in him? Let's examine this.

10

WAITING FOR THE LORD

M odern society may be superior to past generations in some important ways, but there is one area where we seem to have moved backward. We aren't nearly as *patient* as our predecessors. Everything has to be done *yesterday*. Just look at how big a part time plays in advertising consumer products. We now have one-hour dry cleaning, sixty-second rice, and even eight-minute abs! As Carly Simon used to sing (which was appropriated by 1980s aspirin commercials!), we simply "haven't got time for the pain." Unfortunately, we haven't got time for much else either, even important things like children, relationships, and God. Everything is faster now that it was, and as a society we simply don't put up with waiting. Ours is a society of immediacy.

Some might say this is a good thing. We are more aware of the value of time, and we find it unacceptable that others waste our time (though we seem to have no qualms about wasting our own!). As businesspeople understand, time is money. If things can be done quickly, why wait around uselessly?

Yet some things simply do take time. Study, for example, requires assimilation over time. There is no comparison between cramming all night for a final exam and spending a full semester absorbing the material. Though the test results might be similar, a month later the crammer will have forgotten most of what he memorized while the patient studier will have retained nearly everything he learned.

Relationships, too, take time. Friendships are built over weeks, months, and years. There is no speeding up the process. Experiences lived together, misunderstandings overcome, joint ventures carried out, rifts reconciled, confidences shared—all of these ingredients combine to make a deep friendship. There is no quick fix to substitute for the maturing process.

We often hear it said that people's attention spans are getting shorter and shorter. We find it harder to focus on a single project and need to be doing several things at once. A 2005 Kaiser Family Foundation media study asked disturbing questions about children today and the effects of a fast-paced media environment. "Are their developing brains becoming hard-wired to 'multi-task lite,'" the study queried, "rather than learn the focused critical thinking needed for a democracy?" A *USA Today* article by Marilyn Elias reported on this study, noting that the problem intensifies after third grade, when harder coursework requires children to concentrate. The article quotes Susan Ratteree, who supervises other public-school psychologists in suburban New Orleans, as saying that diagnoses of attention-deficit/hyperactivity disorder (ADHD) "have gone through the roof," adding that although the disorder is more recognized these days, "children seem to be different too."[1]

This can be problematic for both our human relationships and our friendship with God himself. Patience is a biblical virtue. Throughout the Psalms we are enjoined to hold fast in attending the Lord's coming, as we read in Psalm 27: "Wait for the LORD, take courage; be stouthearted, wait for the LORD!" (v. 14 NAB). Waiting requires courage; it requires "stoutheartedness"! If we will not wait, we will not receive the many blessings the Lord intends for us. The Lord is not a God of quick fixes and fifteen-minute spiritual tune-ups, but a God of long-term, and indeed *eternal*, promises.

As a college student, I was obliged to read the drama *Waiting for Godot* by the Irish playwright Samuel Beckett. It is a two-act play that deals with a pair of men—Estragon and Vladimir—who spend two full days expectantly waiting for a mysterious figure named Godot, who in the end never shows. It deals with the tedium and frustration of waiting, as well as with the expectation that ebbs and flows over time. Some have interpreted the play as addressing man's life on earth, and his longing for a divine salvation that seems not to come, a God who never reveals himself.

The apostle Paul famously wrote that "love is patient" (1 Cor. 13:4). In fact, of all the possible qualities of love that Paul could come up with—such as kindness, endurance, and devotion to the truth—the very *first* on the list was patience. Love that is not patient is not true love. Paul said the same thing about hope. Like love, hope requires patience. "In hope we were saved," Paul wrote. "Now hope that is seen is not hope. For who hopes for what is seen? But if we hope for what we do not see, we wait for it with patience" (Rom. 8:24–25).

Two of the most important Christian virtues—hope and love—depend on patience for their existence. In the end, we cannot possibly trust God if we will not wait for him, since trust implies the willingness to endure over time. Why, then, is it so difficult to wait? And why would a good and loving God make us wait, rather than answering us immediately?

WHY SO HARD?

Patience is tough for all of us. Many of you have had an experience similar to the one I am about to narrate. When I was a child our family vacations mirrored in many ways the stereotypical holidays of Middle Americans in the 1970s. Mom and the kids would spend hours loading up the family car and then pick up Dad at work in order to leave together on the long road trip. On a good day, the 780-mile drive from Highland Park, Michigan, to Woods Hole, Massachusetts, would take twelve to thirteen hours, not including stops. Some years we would stay over at a motel midway. Other years, when my parents were feeling more adventuresome, we would drive straight through.

We would cut across Canada to avoid the long southern detour around Lake Erie. And it was the Canadian stretch that really got to us. It seemed to go on *forever*. The particular vacation I am thinking of involved a dark green 1973 Dodge maxi van, *sans* air-conditioning. It must have been about three o'clock in the afternoon and we were somewhere out in the middle of godforsaken Ontario, driving along the interminable Highway 401, when the first little mouth uttered the immortal words, "Dad, are we there yet?"

Now the first time that these five words cut through the stuffy, peanut-butter infested air, they evoked a gentle, matter-of-fact response. "No, Mike, we're not there yet. It will be some hours yet." This was not, however, the last we were to hear of those words. My three brothers and I took to repeating the little phrase with antiphonal regularity about once every fifteen minutes, until my parents eventually lost all patience, stopped the car, and informed us that the next child to ask that particular question would get out and walk the rest of the way.

Waiting for something to happen and the tedium it can cause is a universal human experience. The unfulfilled expectation of getting somewhere, or for someone to arrive, or for the phone to ring can be an agonizing affair. We all have known what it is like to sit around anxiously as the minutes spent waiting seem to turn into hours. The torture is compounded when we start questioning whether what we are waiting for will ever happen at all. *Maybe they got lost on the way! Maybe they had a car accident! Maybe they never intended to come at all!* Our imaginations can run wild in these situations.

This happens in our spiritual lives as well. An emblematic case can be found in the Gospels. Do you remember the story of Elizabeth and Zechariah, the couple described by Luke at the very beginning of his Gospel account? Luke portrays the couple as the finest of people, "righteous before God, living blamelessly according to all the commandments and regulations of the Lord" (Luke 1:6). Zechariah was a priest, and his wife, Elizabeth, was a descendant of Aaron (Moses' right-hand man). There was only one problem in this otherwise idyllic scene: they had no children and they were now elderly. The Israelites considered children God's greatest blessing and a mark of his favor. Being barren was cause for shame and a social disgrace. Despite their piety, God had not blessed Elizabeth and Zechariah with children

One day, out of the blue, an angel appeared to Zechariah when he was offering incense in the sanctuary of the Lord. As you would expect, at the sight of the angel, Zechariah was absolutely terrified and recoiled in fear. But the angel tried to calm him with these words: "Do not be afraid, Zechariah, for your prayer has been heard. Your wife Elizabeth will bear you a son, and you will name him John. You will have joy and gladness, and many will rejoice at his birth" (Luke 1:13–14).

To this wonderful message of the most profound joy, Zechariah responded quite unexpectedly. Rather than accept the news with euphoria, Zechariah looked at the angel with skepticism, as if he were playing a joke on him. "How will I know that this is so?" he questioned. "For I am an old man, and my wife is getting on in years" (Luke 1:18). The angel was taken aback at this ungrateful response, and for his disbelief Zechariah was struck dumb until after the birth of the child.

But let's look more closely at what was going on here. The angel didn't announce some bizarre turn of events, like Zechariah sprouting wings or Elizabeth being named Roman procurator. He proclaimed a perfectly ordinary occurrence for a married couple: they were to conceive and bear a son. Moreover, the angel (whose name was Gabriel) prefaced his announcement with these important words: "Your prayer has been heard." In other words, Zechariah should have been expecting this event! He and Elizabeth had been asking God for it, probably every day since they had gotten married. This was simply the answer to their prayers.

So why the skepticism? Why the doubt? Probably because they had simply gotten tired of waiting for God and had concluded that he was never going to answer their prayer. We can imagine that in the early days after their wedding they prayed for children almost as a formality, supposing this would naturally be the case. As the months went on, their prayers undoubtedly grew more fervent . . . and more anxious. As the months turned to years, their prayers evolved as well, sometimes in ardent hope for a miracle, at other times as an expression of near-desperation. But somewhere along the way, those ardent prayers faded in intensity and became a mere convention, a rote repetition of words with no real hope behind them. Their minds turned to other things.

So when Gabriel stated that Zechariah's prayer had been heard, Zechariah had to rack his brain trying to figure out what the angel was talking about. *What prayer? Oh, that prayer. Do we even still say that every night before we go to bed? I had almost forgotten.* And he did not believe. He could not believe. He had long since stopped hoping that God would ever respond.

IMPATIENCE AND PRIDE

So back to our original question: why is patience so tough for us—why is it so hard to wait? Maybe it's just because we are so used to getting things quickly. We have lost our ability to hold out for something better. We want immediate results. But I think there may be another, deeper, moral reason as well. It has to do with pride. We unconsciously think that no one—not even God—has the right to make us wait. Though we may not frame things in these terms, our reaction can be something like this: *Who does God think he is? Who is making me wait? I have important things to do, and he is holding me up.*

I have to make a little confession here. I am, in modern terms, "punctuality challenged." That is, I am frequently late. Not terribly late, mind you, but late nonetheless. I have a lot of excuses. Sometimes I just fall back on the old "fashionably late" pretext, as if people not only didn't expect me to arrive at the prearranged time, but it would be downright inconsiderate to do so! Other times I blame it on the traffic, which often has good grounds in Rome. Sometimes my rationalizations get deeper. I speak about using my precious time well (up to the last minute!), which has the regrettable side effect of occasional tardiness. Besides, since the other person might be late anyway, we'll probably arrive at the same time.

Recently, however, I have begun to make some progress in this area. Though I am still no paragon of promptitude, I have registered discernible baby steps in the right direction. This improvement has been due in part to a painful realization. Habitual tardiness is the fruit of pride! Wait—you may be saying—isn't that a bit much? Isn't lateness a consequence of disorganization and absentmindedness? Why pride? The reason is this. When we keep another person waiting, we are establishing a hierarchy of importance between that person and ourselves. We are telling the other person that our time is more valuable than his or hers and that we are more important than he or she is.

Just think about this for a moment. If you had an appointment with the president of the United States, you certainly wouldn't expect to show up at the White House to find him in the receiving room waiting for you!

Protocol would dictate something else entirely. You would be told to arrive well ahead of the appointed time, and when everything was in place—including you—a secretary would inform the president so that he could see you when he was darn well ready. It is simple etiquette that a person of lesser dignity wait for a person of higher dignity. Habitual lateness, then, reflects an unspoken assumption that our dignity is higher than that of the people we are to meet. This is pride. Ouch!

> *The hardest thing about trusting in God is letting Him respond in his own time.*
>
> —ELIZABETH, AGE 19

So what does our impatience say about our relationship with God? It says that we expect him to arrange his schedule around ours. We want him to conform to our calendar and bend to our timetable. He can (and inevitably does!) wait for us, but woe to God if he makes us wait for him! We won't stand for it. Like little children, we grouse and whine about God not loving us anymore. We wonder what motives he could possibly have for keeping us waiting.

WHY GOD DELAYS

The well-known cry of biblical Israel—*How long, O Lord?*—continues to resonate with us today. Whether it be awaiting a cure for a disease, an answer to our doubts, or assistance to grow in virtue, waiting on the Lord is never easy. We want a response now. *No, ma'am, I will* not *wait on the line! No, Lord, I will not wait any longer! If you truly loved me, you would answer me now!* In the Psalms we read:

> How long, O LORD? Will you forget me forever?
>   How long will you hide your face from me?
> How long must I bear pain in my soul,
>   and have sorrow in my heart all day long?
> How long shall my enemy be exalted over me?

> (13:1–2)

Who among us has not had cause at some point to recriminate God for his slowness in acting? Who has not become exasperated when an answer is needed and needed now?

Yet God's delays are nothing new. If you think God has singled you out for the slow treatment in his request fulfillment, think again. There simply is no express line. Never has been. Remember Jesus' strange behavior when his dear friend Lazarus was sick and died. As you will recall, Lazarus had fallen deathly ill. His sisters, Martha and Mary, sent word to Jesus, "Lord, he whom you love is ill" (John 11:3), underscoring Jesus' affection for Lazarus and trying to move him to quick action. Then the Gospel writer adds still more drama to the scene, reiterating that "Jesus loved Martha and her sister and Lazarus" (v. 5).

But in spite of this love and the urgency of the request, Jesus intentionally tarried two more days before going to Bethany. The Gospel of John stresses how much Jesus loved Lazarus, in part to allay any possible doubts that Jesus' delay stemmed from a lack of concern or interest (our first doubt when God is slow in answering our prayers). It wasn't for lack of love that Jesus delayed. There must have been another reason.

When Jesus arrived late, in fact, Lazarus had already died. This seemed intolerable to Martha and Mary, and they both reproved Jesus for his insensitivity, using the identical expression: "Lord, if you had been here, my brother would not have died" (John 11:21, 32). Both Martha and Mary knew that Jesus could have done something if he wanted. He could have prevented their brother's death. But he didn't! They wanted Jesus to know that they didn't understand. Even some of the onlookers repeated the same thing: "Could not he who opened the eyes of the blind man have kept this man from dying?" (v. 37). All he had to do was move a little faster!

How many times do we feel exactly this way! We believe that Jesus loves us, yet he acts in a strange way. He seems not to come through for us. He delays rather than coming immediately to our aid. He acts unconcerned and even callous. He lets bad things happen that he could surely prevent. We know that he could do something, and we cannot understand how he would choose not to intervene if he truly loves us. *Why would God do this? What possible reason could he have for making us wait? Why doesn't he respond immediately to our needs and requests?*

Yet in our heart of hearts, as painful as it is, we realize that God must have reasons for acting like this. We realize that if he doesn't respond as quickly as we would like, it must be for some greater good. In fact, in the story about Lazarus's death, Jesus says to his disciples point-blank: "For your sake I am glad I was not there, so that you may believe" (John 11:15). In this case at least, Jesus' slowness proved the occasion for his disciples to grow in faith.

But there are other reasons as well. The great Saint Augustine offers the following reflection:

> The entire life of a good Christian is in fact an exercise of holy desire. You do not yet see what you long for, but the very act of desiring prepares you, so that when he comes you may see and be utterly satisfied.
>
> Suppose you are going to fill some holder or container, and you know you will be given a large amount. Then you set about stretching your sack or wineskin or whatever it is. Why? Because you know the quantity you will have to put in it and your eyes tell you there is not enough room. By stretching it, therefore, you increase the capacity of the sack, and this is how God deals with us. Simply by making us wait he increases our desire, which in turn enlarges the capacity of our soul, making it able to receive what is to be given to us.[2]

Augustine concludes that God makes us wait in order to stretch and expand our desire for good and holy things—our desire for him. Here, too, we run into an important concept called "God's time." We've heard of it before. It refers to the moment that God thinks is most opportune for something. Unfortunately, it usually doesn't coincide with our time. When God says, "My ways are not your ways" (Isa. 55:8 GOD'S WORD), he is undoubtedly referring in part to his chronology.

Jesus, on the other hand, was very much in tune with God's time. He was aware that God held the clock. Remember how he refers in the Bible to his "time" and his "hour"? When his mother, Mary, suggests that Jesus intervene to help out the newlyweds in Cana who have run out of wine,

Jesus responds that his "hour" has not yet arrived (John 2:4). When Jesus' brothers suggest that he leave Galilee to go up to the Festival of Booths in Judea, in order to let his miracles be witnessed by more people, Jesus replies that his "time" has not yet arrived (John 7:6). It is only when preparing for the Last Supper before his death that Jesus says, "My time is near" (Matt. 26:18). Moreover, he advises his followers to always be awake and ready, because we know neither the day nor the hour of his arrival (see Matt. 25:13).

THE "APPOINTED TIME"

A biblical concept closely tied to Jesus' "hour" is the idea of "the appointed time." "Appointed" here means predetermined by God, the moment he has chosen from all eternity for a certain event to take place. A great example of this is Jesus' meeting with a sick man at the Jerusalem pool called Beth-zatha (see John 5:1–14). The Gospel says he had been waiting there for an incredible thirty-eight years! From time to time an angel would stir the waters of the pool, and the first person into the pool after the disturbance was cured of any malady from which he suffered. But this poor fellow had been waiting by the pool for thirty-eight years, and every time the water moved, someone else got into the pool before him. By any standard, this would be an exasperating enterprise.

Then one day—when he least expected it—Jesus happened by. For Jesus, however, it wasn't a chance meeting. It was *his hour*, the appointed time. For Jesus it was an *appointment*. It was the precise hour he had planned from all eternity. In Tolkien's brilliant trilogy *The Lord of the Rings*, young Frodo Baggins accuses the wizard Gandalf of arriving late. Gandalf's reply mirrors a truth about God's relationship with us. Gandalf says, "A wizard is never late. He always arrives precisely when he means to." This is the way it is with Jesus. What we might be tempted to call God's tardiness, he would call "the appointed time."

Think for a moment what would have happened if the man at the pool had gone home the day *before* Jesus arrived. "Nope," he would have announced to his friends and family, "it didn't work. I got tired of waiting and finally gave up. Nothing was happening." He would have missed out on God's hour in his life by one day, all because he no longer hoped, no longer trusted.

But upon his arrival, Jesus didn't cure him immediately either. Instead he asked a curious question: "Do you want to be made well?" (John 5:6). A very strange thing to ask, seeing the state of the man and the fact that he was waiting by the pool. Why did Jesus ask this? Maybe he intended to make the man reflect a bit, to reawaken his desire to be well. Perhaps the man was stalled in a holding pattern. Maybe he had gotten used to being the sick guy by the pool and could no longer imagine what it was like to be well, like those prison inmates we hear about who after a while prefer being in prison to being out in the world. Jesus' words make us think, too. *Do I really want what I ask for? Or am I happy the way things are?* Maybe we really don't. Maybe our petition is halfhearted.

God not only has his own time; it often seems to be the worst time. We would like advance warning, a little indication of his plans, some chance to prepare ourselves and choose the best moment. That's not the way it is. Let me give you another example from the Gospels.

Do you remember the time the apostles were out rowing on the Sea of Galilee, trying desperately to cross the water despite the tremendous tempest raging around them? They had been rowing desperately all night, making precious little progress against the elements. Then suddenly, through the lashing rain, they saw Jesus approaching, walking on the water. The apostles were terrified, thinking they were seeing a ghost. Jesus assured them that it was he, and that they had no cause for fear, but they continued to scream out in terror. To the horror of the other, more prudent disciples, Peter shouted out to Jesus: "Lord, if it is you, command me to come to you on the water" (Matt. 14:28). "Come," Jesus responded (v. 29).

Now, by any measure, this was not the best moment for Peter to test out his sea legs. If he really had to walk on the water, why not wait for a calm, sunny day to try this exercise somewhere close to shore? Why the middle of the deep sea, with a thunderstorm crashing upon him?

In our own lives the moments we are called to trust God often resemble

Peter's. They are the moments of greatest turbulence, when everything is out of control. When the kids (or *that* kid!) seem not to listen anymore, when love seems to have gone from the marriage, when every job offer falls through, when our health takes a serious tumble . . . That is when Jesus walks on the waters of our sea, apparently ready to pass us by, unconcerned with our desperate plight. Like the apostles, we can cower fearfully in the security of our little familiar boat. Or, with Peter, we can call out to Jesus: "Lord, if it is really you, call me to come across the water to you!" And we will hear him respond without hesitation: *Come!*

But look still more closely at Peter's trust. He had many ways to ascertain whether it was indeed the Lord, without ever getting out of the boat. He could have said, "Lord, if it is really you, tell me my mother's maiden name." "If it's you, Lord, tell me what I had for breakfast this morning." But Peter didn't do this. He said something infinitely more foolish and infinitely more beautiful: "If it's you, *tell me to come to you across the water.*"

Peter wanted to risk, not because he loved risk, but because he wanted to trust. He wanted to commit himself. He wanted to take a step out. That is why, when Peter began to doubt, feeling the ferocity of the wind and waves, he did not dive back toward the boat the way a "sensible" man would do. No, he threw himself on Christ.

This is when mere belief becomes trust, or when *intellectual* belief becomes *existential* belief. Whether or not the figure walking toward them was Jesus became for Peter more than an academic question. It touched his very life. Mere intellectual belief will never move us, never get us out of the boat. Many people today debate the existence of God. Many who affirm his existence in theory live in practice as if he didn't exist. What good is a faith like that? True faith involves risk. True faith involves an investment of ourselves. True faith involves trust.

God doesn't want us to play it safe. He doesn't ask us to trust only as a last resort, when we have nothing more to lose. He wants us to trust when we have *everything* to lose. Ask yourself: *How much have I really risked on God in my life? How much have I bet? How much have I invested?*

In the Scriptures Jesus issues a most difficult challenge. He says, "Those who lose their life for my sake will find it" (Matt. 10:39). "Losing one's life" means more than going to church on Sundays. It means more than an occasional prayer or a pious thought. It means throwing in one's lot with Jesus and standing or falling with him. It means putting all your eggs in one basket. Have you *lost your life* for him, or are you still clinging to your life, hoping to have both God and the world?

It is a beautiful thing to see young people give their lives to God. When they have their whole lives before them, with a range of possibilities, they choose to serve the Lord. What a powerful testimony this is! Of course it is marvelous to serve God at any point in our lives, but there is something particularly moving about seeing a young person who "throws it all away" for God.

Many try to dissuade them from giving everything up. Others warn them not to waste their youth. Many counsel them to "live" for a while, experience things, and then perhaps serve the Lord in a total capacity. But they refuse. They don't want to give God the leftovers of their lives. They want to give him the very best: their best years, their strength, their youthful vigor, their all.

I'm sure you must have seen the television game show *Jeopardy* at some point in your life. Do you remember how the scoring goes? Players accumulate wealth on account, and in the final round they must determine how much of that accumulated wealth they are going to bet on the last question. In the end, this round usually makes or breaks the players and determines the winner.

These young Christian heroes who throw in their lot with Christ are like those *Jeopardy* players who gamble it all. They don't strategize and calculate, betting the bare minimum. They put everything they have on the line.

GOD'S PATIENCE WITH US

The Christian life is all about the long haul. It more closely resembles a marathon than a fifty-yard dash. Remember Jesus' reference to seed that falls into shallow soil covering rocky ground. The seed sprouts up quickly but just as quickly dries up and bears no real fruit. "The ones on the rock," says Jesus, "are those who, when they hear the word, receive it with joy. But these have no root; they believe only for a while and in a time of testing fall away" (Luke 8:13). The rich earth that is truly fruitful represents those who "bear fruit with patient endurance" (v. 15). Growing roots takes time. It takes patience. And therefore Peter enjoins us: "Do not ignore this one fact, beloved, that with the Lord one day is like a thousand years, and a thousand years are like one day. The Lord is not slow about his promise, as some think of slowness, but is patient with you, not wanting any to perish, but all to come to repentance" (2 Pet. 3:8–9).

When I think of how I resisted God's grace for so many years I can hardly believe it. He pursued me, but I wanted none of it. I wanted to live my life and I didn't want God telling me what to do. How ungrateful and spoiled I was! I don't know how he was so patient with me. I'm just glad I didn't die at that time of my life, because who knows what would have happened. God's incredible patience has to be the greatest gift he has given me.

*—*MARGARET, AGE 52

This beautiful passage from Peter's second epistle reveals some significant truths about waiting for God that may not be immediately apparent. What seems to be *our* patience in waiting for him turns out to be *his* patience in waiting for us! He is waiting for us to come around rather than show up too early and catch us unprepared. Along with increasing our faith and stretching our desire, God allows time for us to repent and believe in him.

Sometimes we focus so much on how long we have to wait for God, we forget how long he has to wait for us. True, we have to be patient with God, but how much more patience must he exercise with us? For every time I can say, "How long, Lord?" He can say to me a thousand times, "How long, Thomas?" We find this in the Gospel of Matthew, too. When the disciples are unable to cure an epileptic boy, Jesus exclaims: "You faithless and perverse generation, how much longer must I be with you? How much longer must I put up with you?" (17:17). God doesn't ask us for a patience that he is unwilling to exercise with us—he exercises it in spades! In fact, he is far more patient with us than we are with him, or with other people, for that matter.

You probably have certain people with whom you have trouble being patient. I know I do. Let me give you an example. Nowadays I travel a lot, especially by plane. I like to travel. I have my routine. I have a little "kit" that includes hand sanitizer, a Bible, Sudoku puzzles, my breviary, laptop computer, newspaper—the works! I know how to divvy up my day to make the time pass. I pray for a while, listen to some music, do a puzzle, read, do some writing, and so forth.

But every once in a while I get seated next to a "talker." You know the kind I mean. A gabber. A Chatty Cathy or a Garrulous Greg. Now don't get me wrong. I am as sociable as the next guy. I enjoy a good conversation and try to take advantage of "chance" meetings for some mutual human and spiritual benefit. But not on planes. On planes, I prefer unsociable people who simply go about their business, perhaps grunting their names as we first sit down with no more conversation until they grunt a good-bye as we part ways.

Being trapped on a plane next to a "talker" first makes me nervous, then anxious, then downright panic-stricken. *Why won't she stop? Isn't he tired yet? Didn't he bring a magazine along? Should I suggest a movie? Would it be uncharitable to discreetly pull out my book and start reading?* I know it is irrational, but that's the way it is. It's a defect. I have no deep or important reason to react like this. It can be something as superficial as wanting to finish my timed Sudoku puzzle or listen to some music.

But God is *never* like that with us. Though we can be infinitely more tiresome and irritating than an innocent "talker," he *always* has interest and time for us. He puts up with our pettiness and inconstancy. He waits for us to come around. He never loses hope or interest in us. No matter how uninteresting or how superficial we may seem, he takes a profound, unflagging interest in us.

The great saint Jerome—known for his wonderful expression "Ignorance of Scripture is ignorance of Christ"—also had something to say about God's boundless patience. He noted that "the Lord is gracious and merciful and prefers the conversion of a sinner rather than his death." And he goes on, "Patient and generous in his mercy, he does not give in to human impatience but is willing to wait a long time for our repentance."[3] It's a good thing he does! Who of us has not benefited from his willingness to wait for us?

In the end, Christ promises us (through a rhetorical question), "Will not God grant justice to his chosen ones who cry to him day and night? Will he delay long in helping them? I tell you, he will quickly grant justice to them" (Luke 18:7–8). He hears our prayers and he answers them, more swiftly than we realize. Our part is to keep crying out to him "day and night," without losing hope. He desires that we implore, that we besiege him with our entreaties. With God, it is a question not of "if" but of "when." He will indeed answer. He will come. He will see justice done.

God's "delays" are one source of stress for those who would put their trust in him and are accepted only by a humble heart willing to let God be God. Other tensions come from ourselves, from our own faults and sins. This obstacle, too, must be overcome with humility, by choosing to place more emphasis on God's greatness than on our misery. In the following chapter we will explore this dynamic more closely.

I I

CAN SINNERS TRUST?

In the end, there are two major obstacles to trusting in God, and I don't know which is worse. The first is the experience of being let down by God and feeling abandoned or misused. The second is having offended God and feeling that there is no way you can trust him again—not because of what he has done, but because of what *you* have done.

It is said that the devil has a very simple approach to driving us away from God. It is a two-part strategy that seems to work quite well, so he seldom varies it. First, he induces us to sin, making evil look fun, cool, pleasurable, and no big deal. Next, once he has gotten us to fall, he plays the part of the accuser, pointing his finger at us and screaming how terrible and unworthy we are, trying to make us despair of ever being saved. It is this second part of the diabolic strategy that I would like to look at now.

When we fail God in little or big ways, we know that something has changed between us. We don't have the same confidence, the same familiarity, or the same spontaneity in our relationship. But this doesn't come from God; it comes from us. Like Adam and Eve, who, after sinning, "realized that they were naked" (Gen. 3:7 GOD'S WORD) and felt ashamed before God, our sin makes us self-conscious and less spontaneous in our dealings with him. Where things were once natural and warm, suspicion and restlessness set in.

I think this is due, in part, to our self-projection onto God of what we expect him to feel. We imagine that on approaching him we will find him cold, angry, and annoyed with us. Even if we sincerely believe in his for-giveness, we may find it harder to believe he can truly *forget*. Like a married couple where one of the spouses has been unfaithful, we assume there will always be an underlying tension, an unspoken loss of intimacy.

Yet our Christian faith assures us that this is not the case. God loves us even in our sin, *while* we are sinning. He doesn't need a "cool-down time" to overcome his initial wrath to be able to look at us again. God never retracts his love. He never withdraws from us because he is fed up or has had enough. He suffers with us. He wishes we weren't sinning. But he goes on loving us with the same intensity, the same totality, the same passion as always.

When God forgives us, he remakes us. He not only glues us back to-gether; he recasts and reforges us so that we are truly made new. When Je-sus promises that he will make "all things new" (Rev. 21:5), he refers above all to our hearts and souls. Lost innocence that we could never regain on our own be-comes possible through the overwhelming power of God's love.

> *How could I not trust God? He has been so good to me. He has forgiven me so much. It would be the greatest ingrati-tude on my part not to trust him now!*
>
> —SILVIO, AGE 54

Not only that, but God even brings good out of our sin. He turns sin on its head and makes it a vehicle for an experi-ence of God's gentle love and penetrating mercy. And so we can really experience the truth of Jesus' words, spoken in the house of Simon the Pharisee in reference to the woman known as a sinner, who had bathed his feet with her tears. "I tell you, her sins, which were many, have been forgiven; hence she has shown great love. But the one to whom little is forgiven, loves little" (Luke 7:47). The experience of God's forgive-ness makes our hearts capable of greater love.

DUST AND ASHES

Unfortunately, knowing these truths with our *minds* and feeling them with our *hearts* are two separate things. We need to allow the truth of God's mercy to descend from our heads to our hearts. Our sinfulness, accompanied by sincere repentance, can even enable us to grow in our trust. It also permits us to purge away old, false reasons for trusting, because along with good reasons to trust in God, there are also bad ones.

For example, we might have operated under the mistaken assumption that God *owed* us his good treatment, and therefore trusted we would receive it. Like the elder brother in the parable of the prodigal son (see Luke 15:11–32), we might have felt that, unlike the rest of humanity, we were worthy of God's appreciation. We worship him faithfully. We obey his laws. We keep ourselves pure. Or in the words of the elder son, angered at his father's seeming unfairness, "For all these years I have been working like a slave for you, and I have never disobeyed your command" (Luke 15:29). It is only right to trust—we may have unconsciously thought—since it is only just that God be good to us.

Perhaps we simply feel that we are better than most. Compared with the rest of humanity we stack up fairly well, so if others have reason to trust, we have more. *God has to be fair, after all, and if he lets them in, he better darn well let me in, too!*

If we assume that God loves us because we are good, we logically suppose he will stop loving us when we are bad. He loved us when we were virtuous, *because* we were virtuous, and he will no longer do so when we act otherwise.

This is one of the greatest temptations we face, a germ that worms its way into our brains and maliciously whispers: "God no longer loves you. He loved you once, but he will not make that mistake again. You are unlovable." It is the devil's most diabolical lie.

But in order to respond we must ask an all-important question: Why does God love us? Why did he ever love us? In the case of human love, there is always a *reason* or a motive for love. "She caught my eye." "He is so funny." "He did so much for me." "She was good to my mother." "We enjoy the same things." In the case of God's love for us, we can dig as deep as we like and never discover in *ourselves* a reason for God to love us. We cannot say, "God loves me because I'm smart," "God loves me because I'm good-looking," "God loves me because I'm athletic," and even less, "God loves me because I'm virtuous." The reason is not in us but in *him*.

The words of the poet Francis Thompson (1859–1907) come rushing forth in all their truth, likening God to a hound of heaven pursuing us, not because of our worth, but in spite of our unworthiness:

> Strange, piteous, futile thing!
> Wherefore should any set thee love apart?
> Seeing none but I makes much of naught (He said),
> And human love needs human meriting:
> How hast thou merited—
> Of all man's clotted clay the dingiest clot?
> Alack, thou knowest not
> How little worthy of any love thou art!
> Whom wilt thou find to love ignoble thee,
> Save Me, save only Me?[1]

Luis María Martínez offers a wonderful comparison to understand this truth. "Let us suppose," he writes, "that a king falls in love with a peasant maid, and because he is in love with her he gives her rich clothing and precious jewels. Who is going to believe that it was the clothing and the jewels that attracted the king to the peasant?"[2] Unlike our love, God's love for us is *completely* free. He loves us because he chooses to love us. He doesn't love us because we are lovable; we are lovable because he loves us.

We must, therefore, valiantly resist one of the most natural tendencies that exist in our relationship with God. When we have the misfortune to offend our Lord in some way, our spontaneous reaction is to withdraw from him and retire into ourselves. We wonder how he will respond when we finally muster up the courage to turn to him again to ask the anguished question: "Do you want me back?" Yet, to this question, the only answer we will ever receive from Jesus is: "With all my heart! I want you back more than I want anything in the world!" God is not like an offended and humiliated wife who must make a herculean effort to receive her unfaithful husband back into her home—if, indeed, she is even able. God does not think twice. He does not deliberate. His heartfelt response is immediate and spontaneous: "I want you back!"

When the prodigal son returns after his villainous ingratitude and countless offenses against his father, he is met not with reproaches but with kisses and a father's warm embrace. He receives not threats, but a feast. And this was not because the father had time to get over his anger; it was because he never ceased loving his son. God merits our trust. And he merits it no less when we have offended him.

GOD'S ILLOGICAL LOVE FOR SINNERS

One of the most consoling themes of the Christian gospel is that of God's mercy. Time and time again Jesus insists on his love for sinners, and that he came to earth specifically to seek out and save what was lost. Perhaps the greatest obstacle to trust in God is the awareness that we don't deserve his love. We try to earn his favor, and when we fail (perhaps even repeatedly) we become painfully aware of the fact that we deserve nothing from God but punishment. In the face of this realization, it can become extremely difficult to continue trusting in God.

We fear that if we look too closely, we may find that we are worse off than we think. How can we approach God for help and count on his assistance when we offend him so often? And yet, our wretchedness, far from disqualifying us, guarantees us God's interest. God reserves a special tenderness for sinners. Christ tells us there is more joy in heaven over one repentant sinner than over ninety-nine who have no need of repentance (see Matt. 18:12–13).

A truth we often forget is that Christ came specifically to save sinners. To avoid possible misunderstandings, he says quite clearly that just as a doctor comes to heal sick rather than healthy people, he has come not to call the virtuous, but sinners (see Matt. 9:13). Far from being an impediment to God's mercy and love, our sins and failings assure us that we form part of Christ's target group. You want sinners? Here I am! Paul exhorts Timothy: "Here is a saying that you can rely on and nobody should doubt: that Christ Jesus came into the world to save sinners. I myself am the greatest of them" (I Tim. 1:15 NJB). Rather than ashamed, Paul was "proud" of this fact since he knew Christ had come for him! Christ's saving mission consisted not of patting good people on the back but of lifting up sinners.

When a beggar seeks to attract the attention of a possible benefactor, he doesn't don his best clothes and strut around as if he hasn't a care in the world. Rather, he highlights his neediness, putting on his worst old rags to show how desperate he is for help. A good beggar knows that it is poverty and want that move a benefactor's heart to compassion. Before God, we all are beggars. Even the best of us can lay little claim to God's love by personal merit. It is our neediness that stirs the King of heaven to take pity on us and shower us with his gifts. At the same time, God is our Father, and every father desires that his children approach him with absolute confidence and trust.

The apostle Paul cries out in confidence about the victory of Christ's love. He asks: "Can anything ever separate us from Christ's love?" (Rom. 8:35 NLT). This is not to say that sin does not effect a real separation from God. Venial sin offends love and weakens our friendship with Christ, and mortal sin—when we knowingly and freely do something gravely wrong—really does separate us from God and destroys charity in the soul (see I John 5:16–17). But God's love is such that even the most heinous sin cannot permanently separate us from him if we are willing to humbly recognize our fault and ask for his mercy.

Look at the "good" thief on the cross. After an entire life of wrongdoing and disregarding God's commandments, one look at Christ was enough to change his heart and move him to defend Christ before his fellow criminal. Then he humbly asked to be remembered—sinner though he was—when Christ entered his kingdom. And the forceful, categorical reply came immediately from Christ's lips: "I assure you, today you will be with me in paradise" (Luke 23:43 NLT).

Some fail to trust because they think they are too far gone. Too much water has passed under the

I came back to church two years ago, and it was as if I had never left. I felt like Jesus opened his arms to me, embraced me, and simply said: "Welcome home!"

—MARIO, AGE 49

bridge, and the time for repentance and trust has passed. A man once said to me, "Unfortunately, I walked away from God years ago. I'm now a long ways away." What the man failed to realize was that God had followed him all those years. Sometimes we walk or even run away from God, yet all we need to do is turn around to find that he is still right there with us. We left him, but he refuses to leave us.

TIME AND TIME AGAIN

The wonderful priest Jean Marie Vianney offered this striking declaration: *"Le plus grand plaisir de Dieu est de nous pardonner"* (Forgiving us is God's greatest pleasure).[3] It is a balm to Christ's heart when he is allowed to pour out his mercy upon us. You will never, ever hear these words from Christ's mouth: "You hoped for too much from me." We never expect too much of God. We always expect too little. God is infinite love. The only thing that holds back the miracles of his grace is our unwillingness to trust in him.

Our immediate rejoinder is: *That may be so for holy people, but I am so bad I have no right to expect so much from him. Not only am I a sinner, but I am an inveterate sinner.* We may object that—unlike Peter, unlike the good thief, unlike the prodigal son—we have not converted once and for all, but even after knowing God's love and experiencing his mercy, we continue to offend him. Perhaps each time we approach Christ to ask his forgiveness we find we have committed practically the same sins we confessed the last time. And we wonder: *Isn't God going to lose patience with me and one day finally say, "That's the last straw. I have forgiven you enough. You have reached the end of your credit line"?*

Fortunately, Christ foresaw that objection and offered a very telling lesson. One day Peter approached him and asked how many times he should forgive his brother who sinned against him—and with a show of heroic generosity he suggested, "As many as seven times?" (Matt. 18:21). And Jesus gently corrected Peter's math and said, "Not seven times, but, I tell you, seventy-seven times" (Matt. v. 22). In other words, as often as your brother comes back and says he is sorry, you must forgive him. Now, if that is the degree of patience and mercy that God exacts of weak human beings, it can be only a dim reflection of the awesome depths of his merciful heart. Again, this is a God who deserves boundless trust, because he displays boundless goodness.

But what form should this trust take? It is one thing to trust God *generally*, but it is quite another thing to expect specific things from him. What is it that we expect from God? Are there things we shouldn't expect? It seems to me that many times people lose faith in God because they expect things he never intends to give. Let's explore these questions.

GOD'S
PROMISES

12

WHAT WE SHOULD *NOT* EXPECT FROM GOD

Does God deliver? Is he to be trusted? This is certainly a fair question, and one this book hopes to shed light on. We should trust people only if they are trustworthy, and this goes for God as well. But in order to know what God delivers, we must first know what he *promises*. It would hardly be fair to judge people's performances by a standard other than what they have committed to. Each must be judged in his field. I mean, you can judge a baseball player by his batting average, but not by his IQ. You can judge a dentist by his expertise in endodontics, but not by his political savvy.

You probably remember a kitschy 1970 song called "I Never Promised You a Rose Garden." It simply asserted that if you were expecting everything to be perfect, then you set up a false expectation that I had no intention of satisfying. Be realistic and be fair. We need to adjust our hopes to what is promised.

To take a mundane example, let's turn to the pizza industry. In 1973 Domino's Pizza introduced its famous guarantee of home pizza delivery within thirty minutes. If a pizza arrived after the deadline, the customer paid nothing. This innovative guarantee allowed Domino's to gobble up a huge percent of the market share, since at the time, no one else was providing a pledge like this. At the same time, the Domino's guarantee was very specific. It promised a speedy delivery but offered no such insurance to cover taste, temperature, or crust quality. *It'll get there on time; that's all we know for sure.*

Again, you cannot complain when the room at your two-star hotel has no private Jacuzzi, or when your accountant is unable to offer good marital counseling. We should expect people to provide what they have offered to provide: no more, and no less.

So what is God's gimmick? What guarantee does he offer? What product does he promise to deliver? Might it be true that we expect things of him that he never promised or intended to give? In this chapter we will focus on the other side of that coin: what God *never* promises. Sometimes—perhaps often, I should say—we feel let down by God because he fails to give what we would like him to give. But there are a number of things that he never offers and in fact sometimes directly denies!

Our first step in honestly evaluating God's trustworthiness consists of adjusting our expectations to his word. If he fails to deliver what he has promised, we are justified in losing trust in him. If, on the other hand, he does exactly what he says he will do, then he is worthy of our confidence.

Of course, technically speaking, there are countless things God *doesn't* promise. He doesn't promise a giraffe for every household, seven days of sunshine each week (except in San Diego), or a red Ferrari on everyone's sixteenth birthday. Then again, very few people expect these things. There are, however, a number of things that people *do* mistakenly expect from God. When these are lacking, the grumbling begins, and trust is easily lost. Let's focus on these for a moment.

GOD'S NONPROMISES

1. PERFECT JUSTICE ON EARTH

One of the biggest complaints against God is the suffering of the innocent. When we look around, we see that no one is spared. Everybody suffers, and sometimes it seems the innocent suffer more than the guilty. It would be easier for us if good people had good lives and the wicked suffered. But this clearly isn't the case. Remember the frustration expressed by the poor psalmist, looking at all the evil people who thrive, with no troubles at all, and so many good people up to their necks in troubles. How can this be?

I was envious of the arrogant;
    I saw the prosperity of the wicked.
For they have no pain;
    their bodies are sound and sleek.
They are not in trouble as others are;
    they are not plagued like other people.
Therefore pride is their necklace;
    violence covers them like a garment.
Their eyes swell out with fatness;
    their hearts overflow with follies.
They scoff and speak with malice;
    loftily they threaten oppression.
They set their mouths against heaven,
    and their tongues range over the earth.
Therefore the people turn and praise them,
    and find no fault in them.
And they say, "How can God know?
    Is there knowledge in the Most High?"
Such are the wicked;
    always at ease, they increase in riches.
All in vain I have kept my heart clean
    and washed my hands in innocence.
For all day long I have been plagued,
    and am punished every morning.
If I had said, "I will talk on in this way,"
    I would have been untrue to the circle of your children.
But when I thought how to understand this,
    it seemed to me a wearisome task.

(Psalm 73:3–16)

The psalmist isn't alone in wondering why things don't seem to work out fairly. Why are good people often "punished," while unscrupulous people seem to get along fine? Consider these well-known words of the prophet Jeremiah:

You are always righteous, O LORD,
  when I bring a case before you.
Yet I would speak with you about your justice:
  Why does the way of the wicked prosper?
  Why do all the faithless live at ease?

(Jeremiah 12:1 NIV)

Why, indeed, do the wicked prosper? This complaint is echoed from generation to generation. We think that God should provide absolute justice here on earth, yet he doesn't. But he never promises to either, does he? He does, however, promise eternal justice, and therein lies a Christian's hope. We believe that the tremendous injustices we experience on earth will somehow be made right in eternity. But not here. Not now.

2. EXPLANATIONS FOR GOD'S ACTIONS

Earthly injustice isn't the only thing we mistakenly expect from God. One of the most typical "prayers," spoken especially by people in distress, is "Why, Lord?" There are many variants of this. We have the self-pitying prayer of "Why me?" and the more selfless prayer of "Why her?" with all sorts of other versions in between ("Why now?" "Why this?" "Why my family?" and so forth). We desperately want to know the *reason* for things, especially *God's reasons* for permitting or willing certain things. We ask him to explain himself, sometimes out of anger, sometimes just because we would really like to know. This is especially true when earthly sorrows seem to contradict God's goodness.

Yet God doesn't like being put on the witness stand and interrogated by his creatures. At least this is what I infer from Scripture and my own experience. If you doubt me, just go back and reread God's tremendous rebuke of Job beginning in chapter 38. After suffering some terrible tragedies, Job dared question God's motives for acting the way he did. This may seem reasonable to us, since by all accounts Job had been treated frightfully, despite the fact that he was a good guy, undeserving of all the grief that had befallen him. But to Job's seemingly reasonable complaint, God replied quite forcefully:

Who is this that darkens counsel by words without knowledge?
Gird up your loins like a man,

    I will question you, and you shall declare to me.

Where were you when I laid the foundation of the earth?

    Tell me, if you have understanding.

(Job 38:2–4)

Rather than answer Job's questions, God simply put him in his place.

Years ago a priest gave me wise counsel that has served me well. He told me that continually asking God to explain himself is an unproductive enterprise. He recommended that every time I was tempted to ask God *why*, I change my prayer to *what*. Rather than ask God *why* he allows this or that, I should ask him *what* he would like me to do. This isn't to say that Christians should never seek to understand God's motives, or that certain prayers are *verboten*. We can be free with God, and ask him—or tell him—whatever we like. The point of this advice was to help me avoid useless frustration and to better focus on what God wants me to do. God rarely tells us just why he does or permits certain things, but he is happy to tell us *what* he would like us to do in response.

> *I wish God would explain himself a little better. People tell me he knows what he is doing, but that isn't so clear to me. If I were God I would do things differently. Honestly his ways seem a little confusing, at least to me.*
>
> —CHANTEL, AGE 30

Part of trust, in fact, seems to be the aspect of trusting that God always has his reasons, even though we don't immediately see them. Like little children who don't understand their parents' actions but trust nonetheless, we are called to believe in him even when we don't comprehend his motives. This can be very frustrating, of course. We rightly wouldn't accept those conditions from anyone else. But God is different, isn't he? He has rights over us that others don't. To attempt to judge God is to reverse the natural order of things and set ourselves up for a terrible fall.

And in reality, we *do* know God's underlying reason for doing or permitting things, don't we? In the end, God really has only one reason for doing things. We know that God is love, and that everything he does proceeds from this love. This is why the saints were able to trust even when things were difficult. They confided in God's love and knew that no matter how bleak things got, God's love would reveal itself victorious in the end.

3. A PROBLEM-FREE EXISTENCE

Sometimes pastors will promise us that God's blessing to his chosen ones is expressed in earthly success. We can measure God's favor in our lives, we are told, by the money we earn, the friends we make, or the upward trend of our careers. Good fortune in this world means that God is smiling on you and pleased with your service, whereas tribulation would mean the opposite. Sometimes this logic is offered in order to win over converts. It is a sales technique. "If you become a Christian, your troubles are over. God will protect you, defend you, and guarantee your investments."

It doesn't work that way.

Read your Bible. Jesus never says: "Stick with me, and you'll have a great time"; "Become my disciple, and your troubles are over"; "For a worry-free life, dial 1-800-JC-ROCKS." In fact, he says something quite the opposite: "If any want to become my followers, let them deny themselves and take up their cross daily and follow me" (Luke 9:23). If a Christian is looking for a smooth, bump-free ride, he is on the wrong track. Jesus said that the road to perdition is wide, easy, and well traveled, while the road that leads to life is narrow and hard (see Matt. 7:13–14). So when things get tough, we shouldn't suppose that we missed a turn somewhere. We are right where we are supposed to be. As Robert Stofel wrote, "God never promised a clean, well-lit resort for our egos, only a lamp for our feet and a light for our path that leads out of this dark world."[1] The "prosperity gospel" that promises big mansions and fancy cars may sound sweet, but it has nothing to do with the gospel of Jesus Christ.

What about fame and friendship? Here, too, Jesus makes no promises. In fact, he warns us that if we sign up with him, things are likely to get ugly. Even though you are familiar with this text, read it again anyway. Jesus said,

> If the world hates you, be aware that it hated me before it hated you.
> If you belonged to the world, the world would love you as its own. Be-
> cause you do not belong to the world, but I have chosen you out of the

world—therefore the world hates you. Remember the word that I said to you, "Servants are not greater than their master." If they persecuted me, they will persecute you; if they kept my word, they will keep yours also. (John 15:18–20)

Jesus makes no bones about it. If we choose to follow him, we can expect the same sort of treatment he received. And we know where that ended—on the cross. Think about it: Is this the way you conceive of your Christian faith? Are you ready to follow Jesus no matter what, knowing that it won't be any picnic?

There are plenty of other corollaries to this *non*promise. In the gospel we find no guarantees of money, praise, good fortune, a long life, good health, an ideal marriage, perfect children, a well-paying job, and so forth. Jesus promises none of these common measures of worldly success, so is it really fair to blame him when we don't get them? Why should we demand that Jesus deliver what he never offered?

A couple years ago I gave my life to Christ. I was completely sincere and completely confident. But if I am honest I would say that my life hasn't really gone so well since then. I expected things to turn around but they haven't. My grades are bad, and my parents got divorced. Something seems really wrong but I don't know what it is.

—KAREN, AGE 18

4. FOREKNOWLEDGE OF LIFE'S TWISTS AND TURNS

This doesn't exhaust Jesus' nonpromises, however. When we sign up for a job, we like to know what is expected of us. We demand a full job description, including our work hours, travel expectations, benefits, vacation time, and future career opportunities. Anything that will be required of us must be spelled out in black and white, up front.

Never try this with God. It doesn't work.

God rarely tells us our futures. He doesn't tell us how long we will live, what difficulties we will face, what sudden turns our paths will take, or even where we will be five years from now. We are on a strictly need-to-know basis, and obviously God doesn't think we need to know an awful lot.

So I suppose it's kind of silly, isn't it, to suddenly turn on God midway down the road and say, "Hey, Lord, I never bargained for this!" Of course not. God never promised to tell us everything. We signed up for a different sort of program and left God in charge of the details.

Remember the call of the great patriarch Abraham and his response of blind trust. God shows up in his life one day and says to Abraham (then called "Abram"): "Go from your country and your kindred and your father's house to the land that I will show you" (Gen. 12:1). Abraham knew not *where* he was going, nor for *how long*, nor *what he was to do* once he got there. God basically said to him, "I'll tell you what you need to know as we go along." Abraham knew only one thing: *who* was calling. He knew that God was trustworthy, so he confided in him.

Do we expect more than Abraham? Do we require a detailed contract written up in triplicate copies, containing everything God will require from us along the way? It won't happen.

Not long ago in Rome I observed a blind man being led by a young woman—probably his daughter. What astonished me most about this scene, besides the utter tenderness of it, was the confidence and sure-footedness with which the blind man strode along the road. He walked *as if he could see.* There was no fumbling, wariness, or missteps. His daughter's eyes were truly his own. It was enough for him to feel her hand to know total security and calm.

I thought, *Would that I had such confidence in God! He truly has me always by the hand, and yet I doubt, I sink, I wander, I pause.* We don't like walking blind. We want to see, so that we can guide ourselves. But what peace comes from allowing God to lead, and from childlike trust in him! Remember the words of the psalmist, comparing God's care to that of a mother cradling her child: "I have calmed and quieted my soul, like a weaned child with its mother; my soul is like the weaned child that is with me" (Ps. 131:2). That's what God is looking for in us!

As a young priest, the great future bishop John Henry Newman wrote a beautiful poem in 1833 called "Lead, Kindly Light," in which he expresses a willingness to be led, without requiring full disclosure on God's part. He did so in the midst of troubling circumstances, having been sick in Italy and unable to travel for lack of a ship. In his own words, Newman described the scene as follows:

Before starting from my inn, I sat down on my bed and began to sob bitterly. My servant, who had acted as my nurse, asked what ailed me. I could only answer, "I have a work to do in England." I was aching to get home, yet for want of a vessel I was kept at Palermo for three weeks. I began to visit the churches, and they calmed my impatience, though I did not attend any services. At last I got off in an orange boat, bound for Marseilles. We were becalmed for a whole week in the Straits of Bonifacio, and it was there that I wrote the lines, *Lead, Kindly Light*.[2]

The poem is not long, just three verses in its original form, so I include it here in its entirety:

Lead, kindly Light, amid th'encircling gloom, lead Thou me on!
The night is dark, and I am far from home; lead Thou me on!
Keep Thou my feet; I do not ask to see
The distant scene; one step enough for me.

I was not ever thus, nor prayed that Thou shouldst lead me on;
I loved to choose and see my path; but now lead Thou me on!
I loved the garish day, and, spite of fears,
Pride ruled my will. Remember not past years!

So long Thy power hath blest me, sure it still will lead me on.
O'er moor and fen, o'er crag and torrent, till the night is gone,
And with the morn those angel faces smile, which I
Have loved long since, and lost awhile![3]

What a beautiful expression: "I do not ask to see the distant scene; *one step* enough for me." In other words, *Lord, you don't need to tell me what's around the next corner; just tell me where to put my foot down next.* God could tell us more—if he chose to—but he doesn't. He intentionally conceals things from us so that we are obliged to trust in him and to walk in his providential care. Begging him to tell us everything or making this a condition of our discipleship is what God calls (to the apostle Paul) "[kicking] against the goad" (Acts 26:14). It is fruitless.

But God is not completely silent about what he expects from us either. We are told little, but just enough. We are told the part we are to play, and what is expected of us *now, today, in this moment.* We are usually not granted a vision of the bigger picture. We must choose either to trust or not. Someday things will become clear.

I remember singing in a choir in high school. The choir was separated into voices, and I formed part of the bass section. On learning a new piece, each voice group would go off separately to learn its part. You may know that the bass part is not particularly exciting. It almost never carries the melody of the song. It offers harmonies that round out the entire piece but doesn't sound very good by itself. So on practicing a new piece, we would have to learn a part that alone sounded quite strange and not altogether sonorous. We had to trust that when inserted into the ensemble of voices, our part would make sense and beautify the whole. And it did.

Our lives are like that. We often look at a *part* as if it were the *whole*, and it doesn't seem to make sense. We expect to be singing the melody, and God has us singing harmony. But taken in unison with God's larger plan for the Church and for humanity, our parts become integral to the loveliness of the whole. Again, God doesn't promise everything. He holds some important things back from us, but he does so with good reason.

5. WARM, FUZZY FEELINGS

A final nonpromise regards our inner selves. We often mistakenly think that even though God doesn't promise us a rose garden, he does at least promise consolations. If we have followed him, we surmise, he must at least reward us with the comfort of his companionship. We expect to feel his presence at prayer and to be filled with light as we trudge along through a world of darkness.

Wrong again. For a Christian, interior consolations are the exception rather than the rule. At the Last Supper, Jesus said to his apostles:

> Very truly, I tell you, you will weep and mourn, but the world will rejoice; you will have pain, but your pain will turn into joy. When a woman is in labor, she has pain, because her hour has come. But when her child is born, she no longer remembers the anguish because of the joy of having brought a human being into the world. So you have pain

now; but I will see you again, and your hearts will rejoice, and no one will take your joy from you. (John 16:20–22)

True, Jesus was speaking specifically about his imminent suffering, death, and resurrection. But in a way, his words here apply to our entire lives. Often it seems that Christians mourn while the world rejoices. We walk as pilgrims in a foreign valley of tears, while others seem quite comfortable and at home. And this pain isn't only external. Often Christians feel empty inside as well. Their faith sustains them, but they often feel nothing, finding no consolation either in the pleasures of this world or in their inmost souls.

Many people abandon God as soon as their spiritual lives start feeling dry or difficult. When prayer becomes hard work, they stop praying, convinced that it isn't for them, or that God no longer has interest in them. Yet again I must insist: Did Jesus ever promise this? Did he say we would always be filled with inner light and feel buoyed up by warm inner consolation? I don't think so.

When we look at the lives of the saints, we see that they were tried by desolation as much as they were calmed by consolation. In this way God purified and beautified them, and now they shine like the stars in the sky. Why do we expect something different? Remember Jesus' tough words: "Brother will betray brother to death, and a father his child, and children will rise against parents and have them put to death; and you will be hated by all because of my name. But the one who endures to the end will be saved" (Mark 13:12–13). For a Christian, patient endurance is often the name of the game. And it will be well worth it: *Well done, good and faithful servant!* (See Matt. 25:21).

If we are expecting any of these five things, we haven't correctly sized up God's promises. He will not guarantee any of these things. In fact, he will most assuredly withhold them from us. If we want to learn to trust, we need to adjust our expectations to God's promises. This is the path to peace of soul and a loving friendship with God.

What *does* God promise, then? What *does* he offer instead? Does he fulfill his word? This will be the true yardstick of his faithfulness. Let's take a look.

13

WHAT *CAN* WE EXPECT FROM GOD?

If God does not promise any of the things we saw in the last chapter, what does he promise? What can we realistically expect from him? At this point you may be thinking that you need to downsize your expectations to fit the reality of God's gifts. After all, if he won't guarantee any of the typical things we look for and dream about, the only option seems to be settling for a more "realistic" view of God, a view that reduces God's action to a minimum. We need to grow up, abandon the idealism of our youth, and readjust our sights to correspond to the way things are. Right?

When in our interviews for this book we asked the question "What can you expect from God?" we received a variety of answers. Some responded that they just hoped God would leave them alone to lead normal lives. Others replied that they hoped for everything to work out all right in the end. A surprising number of people answered that they expect *nothing at all* from God. Some people said this because they really don't think God delivers. Others said so not out of disrespect, but out of *piety*. They said that God doesn't have to answer to us. He has a right to expect things from us, but we have no right to expect anything from him. Besides, some added, his ways are so incomprehensible that we just have to let him act and trust that it is for the best.

Sometimes this attitude seems to derive from people's past unsatisfied expectations. Maybe such people once hoped for many things from God, but experience taught them to expect less. People can get tired of expecting things from God only to see their hopes dashed. So rather than abandon their faith, these people stop expecting anything from God. Over time they trim down their hopes and expectations to the barest minimum. Cynicism creeps in and replaces trust.

Is this our only option? Must we whittle down our hope in God to a more manageable size? I don't think so. Just the opposite: We don't need to *shrink* our expectations; we need to *expand* them. We don't need to expect *less* from God; we need to expect *more*. God promises much greater things than we have ever expected before. Our dreams, no matter how lofty, can never compare to God's amazing plans for us. Paul assures us that "no eye has seen, nor ear heard, nor the human heart conceived, what God has prepared for those who love him" (I Cor. 2:9). Sometimes only by weaning us off our petty desires can God teach us to desire the truly wonderful things he wishes to give us.

> *I usually don't expect specific things from God. Most of the time I don't even know what the best thing would be. What I do expect is that he will always be there for me. He gives me a shoulder to cry on, and the strength to get back up and try again. I don't know what I would do without him. He's really my best friend.*
>
> —JULIE, AGE 34

THINKING BIG

An example from the gospel can help make this clear. When Jesus tells us we are to ask in order to receive and to seek that we might find, he adds an eye-opening illustration. He says: "Is there anyone among you who, if your child asks for a fish, will give a snake instead of a fish? Or if the child asks for an egg, will give a scorpion? If you then, who are evil, know how to give good gifts to your children, how much more will the heavenly Father give the Holy Spirit to those who ask him!" (Luke II:II–I3).

Jesus describes how a good, loving parent will act. Faced with a reasonable request—such as for a fish or an egg—a good parent will give these good things rather than shortchange his child with a snake or a scorpion. Some may suppose that the point of the story is that a loving parent will grant a child's every request. The child asks for an egg; she gets an egg. She asks for a bicycle; she gets a bicycle (and not a toad!). But is this *really* the point of the story? I don't think so. What if we reverse the child's requests. What if, instead of a fish, the child asks for a snake? Or what if, instead of an egg, the child asks for a scorpion? What then? Will she get it? Probably not. The message seems rather to be: a good parent only gives *good* things, not bad.

I remember well that when I was a boy I received many good things from my parents, but they didn't give me everything I asked for. Two things in particular stand out in my mind. Time after time I asked for two things that I never (to this day!) received: a BB gun and a minibike. My parents were concerned that with a BB gun I would put someone's eye out. (This had happened, in fact, with a neighbor of ours.) Regarding the minibike, my dad had seen so many films of gruesome accidents involving motorcycles (he was an automotive engineer) that he and my mom were firmly opposed to my owning one.

The prudence of these decisions could be debatable, and not everyone will agree with my parents' reasoning, but all will agree that they acted out of love, as concerned parents. Good parents don't simply give in to their children's whims; they try to give what is best for them. Jesus is telling us that God is like that. He gives only good things. And just as parents tend to be longer-sighted and more objective regarding their children's good, God understands our needs infinitely better than we do.

Adjusting our hopes in God, then, involves *educating our desires*. It means learning to desire truly good things, rather than immediately attractive things. Just as a young person has to learn that he can't live on chocolate alone but must balance his diet with meat, vegetables, and milk products, so a Christian must learn to aspire to higher things.

People often ask me whether God answers our prayers. He does, of course. He answers all, but sometimes in ways we do not expect. There are petitions that God seldom says yes to. If we say, "Lord, take all my trials away!" or "Lord, give me economic solvency!" or "Lord, make me win the lottery!" the odds are he will answer in some other way. Yet there are other prayers that we know agree with God's will: to become holier, to go to heaven, for the salvation of our family and friends, for the conversion of sinners. These we can count on God answering directly. I dare you, in fact, to try any of the following prayers. These are things God cannot say no to:

1. Lord, give me a deeper sharing in your cross.

2. Lord, make me a channel of your mercy and love to other people.

3. Lord, give me the chance to witness to you today.

4. Lord, make me more like you.

5. Lord, help me to be a better husband [wife].

6. Lord, give me greater generosity with you and my friends.

7. Lord, grant me a deeper knowledge of your will for me.

8. Lord, give me the grace to forgive my brother who offended me.

> *Praying for the wrong thing is like asking your mother for chocolate when you're already overweight. If she gives you an apple rather than a candy bar, she answered better.*
>
> —NATALIA, AGE 22

9. Lord, strengthen my resolve to serve you better.

10. Lord, grant me a greater love for your Church.

All this means that we are called not to diminish our desires, but to *enlarge* them. In the end, we need to be more audacious with God, not less. We need to think big, bigger than we ever have before. Strange as it may seem, we always expect *too little* of God, and never *too much*. The Baptist minister William Carey (1761–1834) used to say, "Expect great things from

t great things for God!" And the beautiful saint Thérèse of
that we should "expect all things from the good God just as
_xpects all things from her father." Instead of reducing God
to the measure of our littleness, we need to magnify our desires to the
measure of his greatness!

GOD'S GUARANTEES

So, getting down to brass tacks, what can we practically expect from God?
What are these "bigger things" he wishes to give us? When I lay out the
list, you may be surprised. It is very impressive.

1. I WILL ALWAYS TELL YOU THE TRUTH

As the saying goes, the truth hurts—at least sometimes. Only a good
friend will always tell you the truth, whether it hurts or not. You can count
on his word because he won't tell you just what you want to hear but will
give you the straight story. Jesus is like that, to the highest degree. So totally does Jesus identify with the truth that he proclaims himself to be "the
way, and the truth, and the life" (John 14:6). Jesus not only *tells* the truth,
he *is* the truth. The truth belongs to his very nature. This stands in sharp
contrast with the devil, the "father of lies." Look what strong language
Jesus uses to describe him:

> [The devil] was a murderer from the beginning and does not stand in
> the truth, because there is no truth in him. When he lies, he speaks
> according to his own nature, for he is a liar and the father of lies. But
> because I tell the truth, you do not believe me. Which of you con-
> victs me of sin? If I tell the truth, why do you not believe me? (John
> 8:44–46)

Jesus said many things to his followers that were hard for them to
accept. He told them tough things, mysterious things, incomprehensible
things. When he told them, for instance, that he was the "bread of life"

and that they would need to "eat his flesh and drink his blood," many of his followers said, "This is intolerable language. How could anyone accept it?" (John 6:60 NJB). His teaching seemed so unreasonable, so obscure, and so downright scandalous that many of his followers began to leave him.

So how did Jesus respond? Did he go running after them and say, "Come back, guys! It was just a figure of speech. I was just speaking meta-phorically. Let me explain"? No. Jesus didn't take back a word he had said, because he had spoken the truth. And when only the twelve apostles were left, Jesus looked at them and asked, "Do you also wish to go away?" (John 6:67). It was—as usual—Simon Peter who answered him: "Lord, to whom can we go? You have the words of eternal life. We have come to believe and know that you are the Holy One of God" (vv. 68–69). As hard as Jesus' words were to understand or accept, Peter knew that he spoke only the truth.

This is exceedingly consoling in our own lives. To know God will never lie to us means we can really trust him. When I was a boy, an aunt and uncle of mine came over to visit, together with a couple of my cousins. We had been told that we could sleep out in a pup tent in the backyard that night. For some reason, my uncle later thought better of it and took back the offer, but seeing us so dismayed at the news, he promised that if we accepted his decision without a fight, he would take us bear hunting the next day. Imagine our excitement! This was too good to be true. I knew absolutely nothing about bear hunting, but it sounded like the greatest adventure imaginable.

We obediently packed everything up and I headed off to bed without a squawk, dreaming about the next day's escapade. Perhaps I should have realized that the promise was incredible and unrealistic, but I didn't. So the next day I leaped out of bed at first light and rushed downstairs for a quick bite of breakfast, with the intention of being ready for my uncle's arrival. Needless to say he never came. His promise had been a ruse to get us to come along quietly the night before.

God isn't like that. Never. He keeps his promises. He is true to his word. We may not always like what we hear, but we know that it is the truth. That means if he says it, you can believe it.

2. I Have Always Loved You and Will Never Withdraw My Love

We have often been told that God's love for us is "unconditional." What does this mean? I think it means that he is not temperamental in our regard. He isn't a capricious lover, one day telling us he loves us and another day telling us to get out of his sight. He does not waver in his love. He never withdraws it. Nothing can destroy or diminish it. In the Bible God says to Israel, "I have loved you with an everlasting love" (Jer. 31:3), and he says the same thing to each of us. He has thought of us from all eternity (before we even existed!), and his love is steadfast and unshakable. We can doubt many things in this life, but we should never doubt God's love for us.

This means that God always wills our good. He wants good things for us, and he wants us to succeed where it counts most. He wants us (in Jesus' words) to "have life. and have it to the full" (John 10:10 NIV). And this means eternal life as well. God passionately desires for us to be saved and to share in his eternal life in heaven. As unlikely as it may seem, God wants to be with you and me for all eternity.

I have met people in this life who have not seemed awfully lovable to me. In fact, on considering whether I would like to spend eternity with them, the answer would be an unqualified no. And I am quite certain that given the choice of a heavenly roommate, many people wouldn't care to spend their eternity with me either. But God would. I know that. That thought alone is enough to keep me going on the worst of days.

God's stubborn love for sinful humanity also means that he will never, ever give up on us. Other people might throw in the towel, convinced that we are hopeless. We may even be tempted to give up on ourselves. God doesn't. He is always in our corner. When we fall down he picks us up again. When we fail he tells us to try again. His "Yes" to us is a yes forever. He never regrets having loved us. He never regrets having created us. He never regrets dying for us. To him, for some inexplicable reason, *we are worth it.*

3. I Will Give You Everything You Need to Reach Heaven

In the end, our most intimate trust in God has nothing to do with money, fame, or fortune. We don't trust in God to make us rich, famous, or popular. Ultimately our trust in him does not concern this life at all. It is a hope in the life to come. Jesus reminds us that it is worth nothing to gain the whole world and lose our souls in the process (see Matt. 16:26). This short life is over before we know it, and what really matters is eternity. Saint Teresa of Avila wryly compared our life on earth to "una mala noche en una mala posada" (a bad night in a bad hotel). What kept her joyful and enthusiastic was the thought of eternity.

As we look around us, we see that no final justice exists in this world. The good suffer, evil often triumphs, and the scales of justice rarely level out. The benefits of Christianity are especially for the world to come. "If for this life only we have hoped in Christ," wrote Paul, "we are of all people most to be pitied" (1 Cor. 15:19). It is only from the perspective of eternity that the things of this earth acquire their true proportion and value.

This means that, for Paul, everything had to be judged by its relationship to eternity. This isn't easy to do! We readily get caught up in our short-term goals, and eternity seems a very long way off. Yet in the end, heaven is the true objective of our existence. So Paul writes, "I am not ashamed, for I know the one in whom I have put my trust, and I am sure that he is able to guard until that day what I have entrusted to him" (2 Tim. 1:12). Paul trusted and put his confidence in God, knowing that he would not be disappointed. But this trust referred especially to "that day" when his trust would be forever vindicated.

Similarly, he wrote: "I am confident of this, that the one who began a good work among you will bring it to completion by the day of Jesus Christ" (Phil. 1:6). Again, it is "the day of Jesus Christ," when his final victory is made complete, that the fullness of Paul's hope would be revealed. This eternity-based trust also changed Paul's way of evaluating other things that we consider important, such as pleasure and pain. He said:

We boast in our hope of sharing the glory of God. And not only that, but we also boast in our sufferings, knowing that suffering produces endurance, and endurance produces character, and character produces hope, and hope does not disappoint us, because God's love has been poured into our hearts through the Holy Spirit that has been given to us. (Romans 5:2–5)

Paul's hope in Christ led him to boast even of his sufferings, since they were a means of his resembling Christ, and also because they became "useful" to produce character and to build hope. *Suffering isn't so bad*, he reasoned, *if it brings me closer to God.* The one thing to be avoided at all costs is what separates us from him and jeopardizes our eternal salvation.

This eternity-centeredness was lived by Christ as well. That is why the author of the Letter to the Hebrews wrote that Jesus, "for the sake of the joy that was set before him endured the cross, disregarding its shame, and has taken his seat at the right hand of the throne of God" (Heb. 12:2). Like hope, trust looks forward to its reward. We know in whom we have believed. We trust in his word. The thought of heaven gives us strength to endure trials in this valley of tears.

One of the things we most need to reach heaven is God's forgiveness. None of us can claim to be perfect. Each of us has need of God's mercy. We all fall. We all sin. We all turn our backs on God and his love. True, sometimes our sins are huge, ugly, and obvious. Other times they are small, subtle, and seemingly harmless. But no sin is harmless and no sin is small.

God gives his forgiveness in abundance for those who request it. He pours out his grace on us and strengthens us for the long haul. He gave us his Word, his sacraments, his Church, his Holy Spirit—a bounty of gifts, all to help us reach heaven!

4. I Will Ask of You Only What You Can Give

I had a football coach in high school who was really tough; in fact, he redefined *tough*. He pushed us so hard that sometimes I thought we would break. But we didn't. When I look back on it, I realize that he was very aware of our capabilities and never pushed us beyond our limits. When someone got hurt, he was right there by his side. When we had problems, he was always there to listen. Sometimes we hated him, since he asked more than we *wanted* to give. But he never asked more than we were *able* to give.

And I also realize, looking back, that he pushed us because he loved us, in a fatherly way. He wanted to bring out the absolute best in us, and even to prove to us that we could do more than we thought we could. He pushed us to greatness, and his record showed it. Whenever I talk with old classmates, we look back on that coach with immense gratitude and affection. He was the best and wanted the best from us.

God asks a lot of us, it is true. Sometimes it feels like he asks *too much*. Sometimes it feels as if he will push us so hard that we will break. But in reality he never allows us to be tested beyond our strength, and "with the testing he will also provide the way out so that [we] may be able to endure it" (I Cor. 10:13). God is demanding because love is demanding. He knows us and what we are capable of. Like a good teacher or coach, he pushes us to give our best and doesn't listen to our excuses. At the same time, he is infinitely understanding of our weaknesses and is always ready to have us begin all over again. He is compassionate with us in our sorrows and stands beside us in our need.

Since God never asks more of us than we can give, he also provides all the tools we need to accomplish his will. The most important "tool" he offers is his grace. He lets us share in his own strength, so that in him and with him we become capable of things we would never have thought possible. In fact, we achieve even impossible things in him! How else can we explain the truly superhuman virtue of the saints? Their charity, their humility, their endurance, their generosity, and their courage fill us with admiration. But they would have been the first ones to tell us that it wasn't *their* virtue—it was Christ himself, and his Holy Spirit living in them. It is his grace that enables us to do all things. So Paul admonishes Timothy: "Guard the good treasure entrusted to you, with the help of the Holy Spirit living in us" (2 Tim. I:14).

Do you recall the extraordinary description offered in the Letter to the Hebrews of those spiritual heroes who had come before? It is a powerful testimony to the strength of God's grace and the need for a boundless faith and trust:

> Time would fail me to tell of Gideon, Barak, Samson, Jephthah, of David and Samuel and the prophets—who through faith conquered kingdoms, administered justice, obtained promises, shut the mouths of lions, quenched raging fire, escaped the edge of the sword, won strength out of weakness, became mighty in war, put foreign armies to flight. Women received their dead by resurrection. Others were tortured, refusing to accept release, in order to obtain a better resurrection. Others suffered mocking and flogging, and even chains and imprisonment. They were stoned to death, they were sawn in two, they were killed by the sword; they went about in skins of sheep and goats, destitute, persecuted, tormented—of whom the world was not worthy. They wandered in deserts and mountains, and in caves and holes in the ground. (Hebrews 11:32–38)

This is not just a litany of sufferings and tortures. It is a heartfelt witness to the power of God's grace in human beings. Since Christians know that God never asks more than they can give, they can accept the seemingly gigantic tasks he sometimes puts before them! Since he backs us up with his grace, there is nothing we cannot do. Sometimes it is the very people who seem the least qualified who show the greatest courage in embracing difficult missions. They lean not on themselves, but on the good God who gives them strength for all things.

5. I WILL BE WITH YOU ALWAYS

One of the most mysterious and wonderful promises Jesus ever made was his vow to be with us always. The only thing that is truly unbearable for a human being is to be utterly alone and abandoned. Jesus promised that we will never, ever find ourselves in that situation. We may have to pass through tough times. We may have to suffer. We may be persecuted and ridiculed because of our faith. We may have to deal with sickness and death, and separation from people we love dearly. Yet we will never be alone. Jesus will see to that.

You have undoubtedly been sick before. Maybe you have spent time in a hospital bed, or lain for days or weeks convalescing at home. When we are sick we often desire one thing above all: company. We understand that people cannot always take away what ails us. They can't always make us well. What they can give is their loving, even silent, presence.

The ironic thing is, we often abandon Jesus, yet he never abandons us. Our friendship with him isn't based on justice; it is based on gratuitous love. We are often very callous with him. We prefer everyone's presence to his, yet when everyone else has left us, he stays with us. We tell him to leave us alone to have our fun, but when the chips are down we look for him again, and we find him. We consider him to be a bore, a spoiler, and a party pooper, but when all our other securities fizzle out into the nothingness that they are, only Jesus remains.

> *When I was diagnosed with cancer I truly thought that God had abandoned me. I kept asking him, "Why? Why? Why?" In the end I realized he was there. It was painful and scary, but he was there the whole time.*
>
> —PHOEBE, AGE 42

We never hear from his lips those words he would have every right to say: *Oh, I see! You had no use for me before, but now that you are suffering, you turn to me? My friendship meant little to you before, but now you want me to come running when all your other buddies have left you for more enjoyable company?* No! He is just happy to be with us in our need. We don't know what faithfulness means until we have experienced the faithfulness of Christ.

But—you may be objecting—in reality doesn't he often leave us? Doesn't he often leave us alone to fend for ourselves? Doesn't he suddenly grow silent right when we most need him to speak to us? It is true that we do not see him or experience him the way we would often like. He does indeed hide behind a veil, which can keep us from recognizing his presence. But he is truly there. Faith often strips away the veil that shields him from our sight. Other times he makes himself known with such vehemence and clarity that we wonder how we could ever have doubted.

No, he will never abandon us or leave us alone. He never promised to be evident or immediately visible. What he promised was: "I am with you always" (Matt. 28:20). Even when he seems to be absent, or silent . . . he is with us, *always*.

6. I Will Give Meaning to Your Life

It was the philosopher and philologist Friedrich Nietzsche who said that man can always find a *how* as long as he has a *why*. Nietzsche was wrong about many things, but he wasn't wrong about that. Human beings need meaning. They need to know that things make sense and have value. There is nothing more deeply frustrating and existentially exasperating than absurdity. Remember the horrible, hellish torture envisioned for Sisyphus, the legendary ruler of Corinth? He was punished in mythological Tartarus by being compelled to forever roll a huge stone to the top of a slope only to have the stone escape him and roll back down again and have to start all over—the very definition of absurdity.

If our work is important, no matter how tough it is, we can muster up the courage to do it. If our labors and sacrifices matter, we can find strength to persevere in them. If all our trials and tribulations make some eternal sense and are not lost in the void of meaninglessness, we can endure. This is the gift God gives us: the gift of meaning. Someday, when we look back over our lives in his presence, all things will make sense. Everything will fit.

United to Christ, every human action acquires value. Nothing is small in God's sight; nothing is meaningless. As Jesus said, "Even the hairs of your head are all counted" (Matt. 10:30). All those efforts you made to grow in virtue, all the patience you exercised with your tiresome aunt, all the endless hours spent in your sickbed or jail cell, Jesus redeems them all. He makes them precious. Everything you place in his hands or under his care turns to gold. It acquires eternal value.

This is why Paul admonishes us to do "all" for the glory of God and chooses the most banal examples to underscore this *all*. He says, in fact, "Whatever you do, in word or deed, do everything in the name of the Lord Jesus" (Col. 3:17). Elsewhere he wrote that "whether you eat or drink, or whatever you do, do everything for the glory of God" (I Cor. 10:31). All those little things, which can seem so meaningless in themselves, have value in Christ. It is God who prospers all things that we entrust to him.

This extends not only to indifferent things, but even to our sins and failings. It is God and only God who is able to bring good out of evil, and perhaps this is his greatest miracle. He alone can redeem our pasts, making them no more causes for shame but pledges of his fidelity. He alone can "make these dry bones live" (see Ezek. 37:1–14).

7. I WILL BE YOUR FINAL REWARD

For Christians, the idea of heaven takes some getting used to. God doesn't offer us a harem of seventy virgins, waiting to care for our every need. He doesn't promise a huge amusement park, barrels of chocolate, or a luxury cruise on the Caribbean. In the end God doesn't promise any*thing* at all. *Things*, after all, can never fill us. Heaven is not a toy store or a garden of delights, replete with everything we could crave or desire. It will not consist in this or that good thing, but in God himself. As Paul reminds us, all the "things" of this world are passing away. The one great promise God makes is to give us himself.

Many people these days dispute the "value" of religion. What does it profit humanity? What has it brought? Is it useful? We wonder whether humanity might even be better off without religion (remember John Lennon's "Imagine there's no heaven"?). Sometimes we may ask the same question about our own lives: *Is God useful? What have I gained from my faith in Christ?* Before you rush to tell me all the real gains Christ has brought you, I would like to challenge the question itself. I don't think God ever promised to be "useful" at all. I don't think the category of "useful" works with God.

I agree that this question has some merit. If we were to find that the idea of God was destructive to human beings and counterproductive for civilization, we would have to think twice about God's existence. Why, after all, would worship of a presumably good God always produce bad effects? Fortunately, this is not the case. Religion, and Christianity in particular, has been a great boon for society and furnished humanity with the most important ideas and principles for building a truly just world. Freedom, human dignity, equality, charity, and universal brotherhood (to name a few of the central ones) are all quintessentially Christian notions.

Yet there is a problem with this whole approach. By asking about God's usefulness, we reveal a notion of God that is *utilitarian* to the core. God would simply be an instrument, or a tool that helps us achieve some other goals. God becomes a *means* rather than an *end*. This distinction may seem like hairsplitting, but it's not. It goes to the heart of what the Christian religion is all about.

The key difference between religion and magic is that magic seeks to harness supernatural powers and subordinate them to our will. Religion, on the other hand, is the worship of God, and the subordination of our wills to his. Magic seeks to *use* the supernatural, whereas religion seeks to adore and to serve.

In the Bible we find a different idea of God. There God is portrayed as the beginning and the end, the Alpha and the Omega. He is not a helpful piece of a bigger plan. He is the overarching truth that gives meaning to life. We come from him and are ultimately going to him. He is not a means to anything bigger or more important than himself (health, financial success, world peace, a clean environment . . .); he is not a *means* at all.

In his book *Jesus of Nazareth*, Pope Benedict XVI asks a very important question and offers an equally illuminating answer. He echoes humanity's question regarding what Jesus gave the world. In many respects, Jesus could be considered a human failure. It seems that none of his efforts brought about lasting change in the world. Jesus healed the sick but did not abolish sickness; our world still abounds with hospitals full of sick people. Jesus gave sight to the blind but did not eradicate blindness. Jesus even raised the dead, but after him people continue to die. Disease and death have not been uprooted from the world. By multiplying loaves and fishes on the mountainside, Jesus fed five thousand men one afternoon, but he did not eliminate hunger and starvation. In our world people still are born poor and hungry and die poor and hungry every day. Jesus likewise forgave sinners, yet people keep on sinning. Jesus did not eliminate sin. Jesus came as the Prince of Peace and preached peace and selfless love to humanity, yet there still are wars, strife, and conflict throughout the world. Jesus did not install a lasting peace.

So what did Jesus give to the world? And Benedict answers quite simply: *He gave us God.* Jesus came not as a solution to our problems, but to give us the ultimate truth we are seeking: God himself. In other words, Jesus did not come as a *useful* Messiah, but simply to show God's face to the world. He was—and is—Emmanuel, God among us.

Of course Jesus also came to save us, to offer us redemption from our sins, and to show us the way to the Father. He sent his Holy Spirit on his disciples and continues to give us his grace and strength to choose good. Yet, in the final analysis, it is union with him that we seek, and not some other good. He is both the *Way* and the *Life*. This is why our age finds it so difficult to imagine or appreciate the idea of heaven. We want to know what reward we get for being good and not straying off the path of righteousness. We would almost prefer a more earthly heaven with pleasures we can understand. But this isn't really the Christian idea of heaven at all. For Christians, the final and great reward of eternal life is God himself. His gifts will pale, and all that will matter to us will be the Giver.

Trusting in God, then, means learning to desire God, to hunger and thirst for him more than anything else. It means believing that he will be our treasure, that he will fill us and satisfy us. To look to God simply as a solution to our problems—an effective means to achieve our goals—is to set ourselves up for major disappointment. God wants to be, and has to be, much more for us. He is heaven itself.

In the midst of our explorations into God's trustworthiness and what we can expect from him, we should also look for a moment at how he trusts us. God is not only trustworthy, he is also *trusting*. Maybe if we get a better sense of how he trusts us, we will have an easier time trusting him. Let's look.

14

*

RECIPROCITY: GOD'S TRUST IN US

G od not only expects trust. He also bestows trust. Without a doubt, this is a very strange thing, when you think about it. After all, we are the most fickle, fragile, and fallible creatures in the cosmos. Yet he does. He commends to weak human beings that which is most precious to him. He entrusts husbands and wives to one another. He entrusts mothers and fathers with the immense privilege and responsibility of cocreating with him and caring for his own children. He delegates to the whole human race the task of caring for his creation: the world and all that is in it. In a very real way he commends each of us to the rest. We are, indeed, our brothers' and sisters' "keepers."

Moreover, by making us free, God entrusts us to ourselves. That is, our final destiny and the fruitfulness of our lives on earth are placed in our hands. This doesn't mean God is foreign to this endeavor. He is right by our side, even within us, strengthening us with his grace and prospering the work of our hands. At the same time, he never violates our freedom or compels us to act against our own will. He invites, cajoles, urges, and commands, but he does not compel. No one enters heaven against his own will.

Freedom was God's greatest gift to the human race, but also God's greatest risk. Our freedom allows us to embrace his love and return it to him, but we can also rebel against him and prefer creatures to our Creator. This was a risky endeavor because God endangers that which is most precious to him, his relationship with us, his children. By letting us out of the sheepfold, God risked having us wander off on the hills, far from the divine Shepherd. And yet this is what he wanted to do. Love that is coerced is no love at all. He made us in his own image and likeness, free to choose him from the depths of our being, but also free to deny and crucify him.

Why did God do this? Because he trusts us. He believes in us. He knows "how low we can go," but he also knows the greatness of which we are capable and the love we can give. Like the best of fathers, God lets us go rather than clinging to us and restraining our movement. You have undoubtedly heard the little saying attributed to Richard Bach: "If you love something, set it free. If it comes back to you, it's yours. If it doesn't, it never was." This is very much how God treats his children. The only difference is that even when we stray he seeks us out, not to compel us to return but to plead with us.

> *When you live with God you learn to trust him and he trusts you. You need to have trust in a relationship for it to work and this trust has to be 100 percent.*
>
> —ANNETTA, AGE 23

In his book *God, How Much Longer?* Pastor Robert Stofel narrates his experience of burnout in his ministry. He simply wanted out. He writes that he even reached the point where he said to God, "I don't even know if I believe in you anymore," only to hear him respond, "That's okay. I still believe in you."[1]

IF GOD TRUSTS YOU, YOU CAN DO IT

From the moment of man's creation, God has entrusted the world to him. Men and women are to "fill the earth and subdue it." They are to "have dominion over the fish of the sea and over the birds of the air and over every living thing that moves upon the earth" (Gen. 1:28). They are to "till . . . and keep" the garden in which they have been placed (Gen. 2:15). From the very beginning God has delegated to human beings his providential care of creation and made them his stewards, his ambassadors.

Jesus picks up on a similar theme in the gospel when he likens his disciples to administrators put in charge of their fellow servants to give them their share of food at the proper time (see Luke 12:42). This is a great responsibility, and one for which the disciples must render an accounting. This is why Jesus concludes his parable of the faithful or the unfaithful slave with the stern warning: "From everyone to whom much has been given, much will be required; and from the one to whom much has been entrusted, even more will be demanded" (Luke 12:48).

But God's trust is not given in vain. He doesn't place impossible burdens on our shoulders only to see us fail. In fact, his trust is the greatest source of our courage and confidence to embrace everything he asks of us. God's trust demands from us a holy audacity in undertaking humanly impossible tasks when it is clear that God is asking them of us. God never accepts inadequacy as a valid excuse for not accomplishing his plans. Rather, it is a prerequisite. What he asks of us doesn't *often* exceed our human capabilities; it *always* exceeds our human capabilities. God doesn't work through only perfect, flawless instruments. If he did, he would have quickly found himself bereft of any suitable helpers for the past two thousand years. What he does require is our humility, goodwill, hard work, and trust. With these elements, we cannot fail. This is because God's trust is accompanied and bolstered by his grace. He gives us everything we need to succeed.

This audacity in taking on all that is asked of us must be accompanied by true humility to know that we are nobody's savior; Christ alone is. It would be deceitful and unfair to lead people to place their trust in us rather than in God. You know the hit song Bill Withers recorded in 1972, and which has been rerecorded by others, titled "Lean on Me." In it he promises to be a friend and fellow burden-bearer for his friends and hopes they'll do the same for him. These are beautiful and noble sentiments. Many times we are pleased to be a support for others and to find our support in them. This works up to a point. We do often find solace, counsel, companionship, and strength in others. Moreover, we often are able to provide strength for others as well, and this is a source of real joy.

Yet it can also be scary. When another person begins to place all of his or her trust in us, we are forced to confront our own weakness and vulnerability. We know that we can provide many things, but we also know that we cannot provide everything, as much as we would like to. In the end, when a loved one is lying sick in bed, or destitute and unemployed, or abandoned by a spouse, we can do only so much. There are wounds we cannot heal and ills we cannot correct.

Here a true Christian knows that he or she is but an intercessor, called to bring others to Christ. None of us can take Jesus' place. Like John the Baptist, we, too, must be quick to acknowledge: "He who has the bride is the bridegroom. The friend of the bridegroom, who stands and hears him, rejoices greatly at the bridegroom's voice. For this reason my joy has been fulfilled. He must increase, but I must decrease" (John 3:29–30). We are, if you will, mere "matchmakers," called to introduce Christ to souls who will find in him their salvation. We are not here to draw souls to ourselves, to gain their loyalty and their love, but rather to lead them to the Bridegroom. We are the Bridegroom's friends, overjoyed when he is known and loved.

And it is precisely this word *friends* that Jesus uses to describe his disciples at the Last Supper. He doesn't want them simply as servants. He wants them to know that he has shared his mission with them, revealing to them everything he heard from his Father. These are Jesus' words:

> I do not call you servants any longer, because the servant does not know what the master is doing; but I have called you friends, because I have made known to you everything that I have heard from my Father. You did not choose me but I chose you. And I appointed you to go and bear fruit, fruit that will last, so that the Father will give you whatever you ask him in my name.
> (John 15:15–16)

Jesus calls us his friends because he trusts us, enough to reveal his most intimate truths to us, enough to depend on us to bear fruit that will last. He calls us, enlightens us, strengthens us, and appoints us to carry on his evangelizing mission. That's how much he trusts us!

I often marvel at how much God has placed on my shoulders. When I was young, I never imagined I would be called to raise seven children and to do the many things I have done. He has asked a lot, and I have tried not to let him down. And he has never let me down either.

—MARISOL, AGE 67

TRUST AS A MEANS OF BUILDING TRUSTWORTHINESS

But the Lord's trust in us has another purpose as well. Sometimes trust is given even when the recipient of the trust doesn't merit it. This may seem strange, since it would seem that trust should always correspond to faithfulness. This isn't necessarily so.

A good example of this is a parent-child relationship where the child—perhaps an adolescent—has not proven to be overly trustworthy. A logical reaction to this would be the removal of trust. We could simply stop relying on the unfaithful child and place our trust elsewhere. But a parent has a long-term goal for his child, including that the child become a mature and responsible adult. Sometimes placing trust in someone who is not worthy can have the salutary effect of helping him or her to rise to the occasion, in a desire to show that such trust was not ill-placed. There is no formula, of course, to know when this sort of measure should be taken. The timing has to be right. Yet, God's dealings with us offer much food for thought here.

God exhibits a sort of "willful blindness" in trusting us. He seems to choose to forget our transgressions. We may fail him time after time, and yet he comes back relentlessly, ready to trust us again. This reminds me of some parents I know who defend their children no matter what. There can be a cloud of witnesses who attest to the child's wrongdoing, and still the mother and father will doggedly defend their child. While such defense may be counterproductive in the raising of children, God often shows himself to be just this indulgent.

Let's take an emblematic example, that of Jesus and Judas. Judas was not trustworthy, and Jesus—who always knew what was in a person's heart (see John 2:24–25)—could not have been ignorant of this fact. Yet of all the possible candidates for the job of treasurer for the apostolic band, Jesus chose Judas. He held the common purse—a position of extreme trust. He kept the accounts, made the disbursements, and received donations, with no checks or balances of any kind. Unfortunately, Judas was a thief, he got away with it, and no one (except Jesus) knew.

Jesus has told his disciples quite bluntly: whoever is faithful in little things will be faithful in greater things; the one who is dishonest in little things will be dishonest in greater things (see Luke 16:10–12). Our trustworthiness does not depend on the magnitude of what is given to us in trust, but on our character. People who haven't been faithful in lesser moments don't suddenly come around when it matters. Jesus' trust in us is given in the hope that we will be good and faithful servants, and still more, true friends worthy of his confidence.

But God's trust in us brings up another important issue. How much are we supposed to try to do, and how much should we leave for God? Does he wish us to be active or simply step out of the way? Are we to be trusting or responsible? Is there any way to reconcile the two? Let's investigate.

15

PROVIDENCE AND PERSONAL RESPONSIBILITY

Trust and personal effort seem to be at loggerheads. It seems we must choose one or the other. The typical reasoning goes something like this. If you work too hard, it means you don't *really* trust in God. If you *really* trusted, after all, what need would there be to put so much effort into things? Didn't Jesus say that we Christians shouldn't worry and fret about so many things, since only one is needed (see Luke 10:41–42)? Didn't he recommend that we let tomorrow take care of itself (see Matt. 6:34)? Didn't he teach us to be like the lilies of the field, neither toiling nor spinning (see Luke 12:27)? Why so much attention to worldly responsibilities, if Jesus wants us to rely solely on him?

From this logic it would seem that the goal of our spiritual lives should be to reach a point of absolute trust and utter inaction. We should sit back, worrying about neither what we are to eat nor what we are to drink, trusting that God will act. We should make no effort to do anything and simply allow God to take care of us. He made the entire universe without us, after all, so he can certainly sort out humanity's problems without us. Yet I think this would be a tremendous mistake. While putting forth no effort at all seems to square with certain biblical passages, it clearly clashes with others. Some interpretation is needed here.

Jesus doesn't compare his followers with only the ravens and the lilies of the field. As we have seen, he also compares them to a prudent manager, who knows how to dispense food to the servants at the appropriate time (see Luke 12:42). He compares them to servants entrusted with their master's money, to administer and "do business" (Luke 19:13). He tells his disciples that the harvest is plentiful and the *laborers* are few, and tells them to "ask the Lord of the harvest to send out laborers into his harvest" (Luke 10:2). Before ascending to his Father, Jesus furthermore sent his disciples out to the whole world to make disciples of all the nations (see Matt. 28:19). Hard work and steady activity seem to be such an integral part of the Christian mission, in fact, that Paul bluntly states: "Anyone unwilling to work should not eat" (2 Thess. 3:10). The example of the apostles after Christ's ascension is one of tireless work for the kingdom of Christ.

> *I was brought up being told that God helps those who help themselves. Christians were supposed to be the light of the world. Now at my church they tell me we need to trust in God to make things right. I really don't know what place trust has in my life, or even what place it should have.*
>
> —KIM, AGE 19

So how can we reconcile these two apparently contrary positions? Are we to work or are we to trust? Are we to take personal responsibility for the mission assigned to us, or are we to sit back and wait for God to take care of things?

WHOSE JOB IS IT?

In the history of Christianity, people have often sided with one or another of these approaches. The more extreme examples have gone under the name of Pelagianism on the one hand, and quietism on the other. Christians have officially rejected both of these dangers during the centuries, yet they sometimes still raise their ugly heads.

Pelagianism, named after a fourth-century monk called Pelagius, stressed the importance of human activity up to the point of denying the need of divine grace for man's salvation. Jesus would have given his followers "good example" without being a redeemer. What matters is human freedom, and how we choose to use it. Pelagians emphasize action over contemplation, personal responsibility over trust.

Quietism, on the other hand, adopts the contrary approach. Here a passive acceptance of all things is preferred over active efforts to change things. The highest value is tranquillity of soul and self-abandonment to God, up to the point of denying any value to human activity. In the end, quietists would say, human actions don't matter; they don't change anything. God will do what he will do, and he laughs at our silly little plans and endeavors, which invariably come to naught.

I think we can see how each of these approaches has something attractive and something true about it. Those who stress activity over contemplation rightly note that each of us has a "mission" to carry out, and that we will be judged on our deeds. Each of us is his brother's keeper and, moreover, must answer for his own soul. God gives his grace but never forces our hand or obliges us to love or obey him. God made us free so that we could love him and serve one another not out of compulsion, but as a personal response to his love for us. God made people free, with the power to choose good or evil, life or death. He put the world in our hands, as instruments of his providence, and we cannot just sit back, cross our arms, and wait for God to do something. Sins of *omission* are just as bad as sins of *commission*.

This is all true, but it isn't the whole truth either.

We also need to realize that God is ultimately in charge, and more things are outside our control than within it. All of us must learn to "let go and let God," a slogan that is pregnant with significance. In the end, it is up to God to sort out human history. He is the Lord. As the psalmist says, "Commit your way to the LORD; trust in him, and he will act" (Ps. 37:5). Rather than exaggerate our own importance, we must cultivate peace of heart and a boundless trust in God. Jesus reprimanded Martha, who wor-

ried and fretted about many things, and
reminded her that only one thing is important. It was her sister, Mary, who sat
at Jesus' feet and listened to him, who
chose "the better part" (Luke 10:42).

> *For me, the hardest thing about*
> *trusting in God is letting go.*
>
> —NATALIA, AGE 22

Which is it, then? Does God want us to be active or prayerful, quiet
as a babe in its mother's arms or full of zeal for his kingdom? Are we to
go out to the highways and byways, proclaiming Jesus Christ to the world,
or should we go to our private rooms and close the door, entrusting all of
human history to God's providential care? Should we build schools and
hospitals, march for human rights, and come to the aid of the poor, or
should we put all of humanity in God's hands, trying to live in purity of
life and peace of heart?

Fortunately, we don't need to make this choice. We don't need to choose
one to the exclusion of the other. It's not a question of trusting God *or*
actively pursuing his kingship. It is *both*. We are called to be trusting in
our activity and active in our trust. Let's look more closely at the dynamic
behind this cooperation.

COWORKERS WITH CHRIST

Though God could be more effective if he worked alone, he rarely chooses
to do this. He prefers the infinitely more challenging path of working
together with us poor, weak, inconstant, petty human beings. He put men
and women on this earth as his stewards, the administrators of his providence. As the Bible teaches, "When God, in the beginning, created man,
he made him subject to his own free choice" (Sir. 15:14 NAB). Through the
use of our freedom, we cooperate both in our own salvation and in the
temporal and eternal well-being of our brothers and sisters as well. This is
a daunting, even terrifying responsibility. We have the immense weight of
the world on our shoulders.

Of course, God doesn't leave us alone to shoulder this burden, or it
would crush us. He is by our side the whole way, fortifying us with his

grace, comforting us with his blessings, enlightening us with his Word, inspiring us with his example. Moreover, in this cooperative enterprise, he bears the lion's share of the responsibility. But he really does choose us to be not only beneficiaries of his redemptive mission, but also coworkers in it. It is no exaggeration to say that he depends on our cooperation for our own salvation and that of many of our brothers and sisters.

The apostle Paul offered some very meaningful allusions to help us understand this relationship. At one point, he compares himself and another apostle—Apollos—to agricultural workers in the Lord's field. Paul was frustrated with some Christians' tendency to take sides with him or with Apollos, as if they, rather than Christ himself, were the founders of the Church. So Paul said,

> What then is Apollos? What is Paul? Servants through whom you came to believe, as the Lord assigned to each. I planted, Apollos watered, but God gave the growth. So neither the one who plants nor the one who waters is anything, but only God who gives the growth. The one who plants and the one who waters have a common purpose, and each will receive wages according to the labor of each. For we are God's servants, working together; you are God's field. (I Corinthians 3:5–9)

Paul sees himself as a planter, a sower. He spreads the seed of God's good news in Jesus Christ. No sower is silly enough to think that the plant grows because of him. It grows because of its interior dynamic. But by sowing, the farmer gives it contact with the soil and an opportunity to grow. Apollos, Paul's colleague, waters the seed to help it grow. Paul announces the good news; Apollos nurtures it along. Yet Paul wants to make clear that the real reason the seed grows is because of God, and not because of God's human coworkers. So he says, "Neither the one who plants nor the one who waters is anything, but only God who gives the growth."

When I was growing up, my mother had placed a small plaque on the wall of the bathroom behind the kitchen. For those tempted to see themselves as indispensable, the plaque provided a helpful reminder. It read as follows:

Once God and I a garden made,

And how our flowers grew!

I gave my share with hoe and spade;

He gave his sun and dew.

I thought myself a needed part of the flowers we had grown,

Until I saw wood violets, that he had raised alone.

Still, Paul isn't ignorant of the need for apostles either! He describes himself and Apollos as "servants through whom you came to believe." This is a marvelous gift and honor—to be called to share in bringing souls to Christ. Paul sees that it was through his preaching that the Corinthians came to believe. Elsewhere, too, he acknowledges the importance of this mission:

> How are they to call on one in whom they have not believed? And how are they to believe in one of whom they have never heard? And how are they to hear without someone to proclaim him? And how are they to proclaim him unless they are sent? As it is written, "How beautiful are the feet of those who bring good news!" (Romans 10:14–15)

Here Paul avoids two errors that commonly plague Christians. One is to think of ourselves as indispensable; the other is to think of ourselves as superfluous. We are neither. We are necessary because God wants us to be necessary. He has woven us into his plan. God could have chosen perfectly well to do things without us. He could do everything himself. But he doesn't want to.

Why, after all, did Jesus gather disciples around him in the first place? Why did he choose twelve apostles and give them special training and a special mission? Why did he tell his followers to go out to the whole world and make disciples of all the nations? Why did he found a Church as a community of believers, called to continue preaching and teaching in his name?

Jesus could just as well have done this all himself. He could have said "Poof!" and had all humanity infused with knowledge of him. Why do things the hard way, where people will fail him? Because that's the way he chose to do it. He wanted us as active coworkers, not passive bystanders.

But Paul's analogy doesn't end with the sower and the waterer. Next, he compares his and Apollos's work to that of masons constructing a building—God's building. So he says,

> According to the grace of God given to me, like a skilled master builder I laid a foundation, and someone else is building on it. Each builder must choose with care how to build on it. For no one can lay any foundation other than the one that has been laid; that foundation is Jesus Christ. (I Corinthians 3:10–11)

He laid the foundation by introducing the Corinthians to Christ, their Lord and Savior. He preached Christ crucified, and they believed. Then Apollos, another fellow builder, continued adding layers and levels atop the foundation that Paul had laid. And the foundation was Christ himself. Christians have always seen in Paul's words an allusion to the Church—God's building—of which Jesus himself is the foundation.

LIVING IN THE PRESENT

Recognizing the need to work together with God as his docile yet responsible instruments, how can we do so with absolute trust in his power and love? How can we work as if everything depended on us, while praying and trusting as if everything depended on God? One key way is to strive to live in the present moment, leaving both the past and the future in God's hands. Trust in God for the future allows us to live fully in the present. We count on him to prosper the work of our hands. He will make our actions fruitful. Focusing on the task at hand, on God's will for you *right now*, allows you to combine personal responsibility with trust in God's providence. "Do not worry about tomorrow, for tomorrow will bring worries of its own. Today's trouble is enough for today" (Matt. 6:34).

There is an old Latin maxim that reads "*Age quod agis.*" It literally means

"Do what you are doing." Keep your mind in the present. Focus on the task at hand. Some spend much of their time lamenting the past or fearing the future, and in so doing they miss out on the one thing that is truly in their hands: the present. If we are sorry for an ill-spent past, the best way to set things right is to act well now. There is no sense wasting today being depressed about what happened yesterday. We ask God's forgiveness and get to the business of loving him in the here and now. Likewise, if we really care about the future, the best thing we can do is dedicate ourselves whole-heartedly to the activity at hand. That is the best assurance that things will be right in the future.

Indeed, as James reminds us, tomorrow is an unsure thing; we may not be around to see it (see James 4:13–15). An accounting could be asked of our lives this very night (see Luke 12:20)! All we truly have is the present moment. The past is gone and the future is unsure. So the real questions for Christians become: *Are we loving God now? Are we doing his will in this very moment?*

So let's say we've decided to get down to the business of living our Christian lives more responsibly and to actively trust in God. What then? What if we've somehow lost our ability to trust along the way? Is there any way to get it back or to grow the trust we have left? Let's look more closely.

MAKING
TRUST
HAPPEN

16

REGAINING LOST TRUST

Though young people rush to become adults, Jesus often invoked the example of little children as a model for Christians to imitate. Too much "adulthood" isn't good for a Christian. No one is a grown-up before God. And thus Jesus called his followers to be like little children, to welcome the kingdom as children would do. You undoubtedly remember this moving scene from the Gospel of Mark:

> People were bringing little children to him in order that he might touch them; and the disciples spoke sternly to them. But when Jesus saw this, he was indignant and said to them, "Let the little children come to me; do not stop them; for it is to such as these that the kingdom of God belongs. Truly I tell you, whoever does not receive the kingdom of God as a little child will never enter it." And he took them up in his arms, laid his hands on them, and blessed them. (10:13–16)

Being childlike isn't easy for adults, especially modern adults. We are educated, freethinking, critical, and sometimes even cynical. This is especially true in the case of trust. Little children trust spontaneously. To reach for Mommy's hand in a moment of disorientation is the natural gesture of a child. Children believe what their parents tell them. They trust in their words and promises. Children do not second-guess their parents' motives or suspect their integrity. But somewhere along the way things change.

Maybe it's because as we grow up we become more and more independent, relying on ourselves more than others. Maybe it's because we have been burned and no longer believe in anyone but ourselves. Maybe it's because our society urges us to become self-reliant and not depend on others. Whatever the causes may be (there are surely many), the older we get, the harder it is to trust.

So what if we find ourselves in the unpleasant—but typical—situation of those who no longer trust or who don't trust as much as they should?

> *I suppose I used to believe in God when I was young. But I guess the older I get the less trust I have. That's kind of sad, isn't it?*
>
> —CARMEN, AGE 56

Can we ever regain what we have lost? Of course we can. Even though it may seem a long way off, Jesus reminds us that "what is impossible for mortals is possible for God" (Luke 18:27).

If you're really serious about growing in trust, you may have to buckle your seat belt for the ride that awaits you. Growing in trust means, among other things, pushing your willingness to risk outside your present comfort zone. It also means some hard work, as you stretch and exercise your ability to trust the way a gymnast stretches and tones her muscles. Yet even in this exercise God will be by your side and within you, helping you through. Our work goes hand in hand with God's grace. Let's see how this happens.

ARK-BUILDING AND GROWTH IN TRUST

God often answers our prayers for greater virtue by sending us opportunities to *practice* the virtue in question. When we pray for humility, God doesn't simply say, "Presto!" and make us as humble as a wooden chair. Rather, he offers us opportunities to practice humility, and he gives us the grace and strength to take advantage of these opportunities. Similarly, when you pray for greater trust, don't be surprised if instead of an instantaneous trusting attitude, God sends you occasions where you will need to trust in him alone.

The year 2007 saw the release of the film *Evan Almighty*, a sequel to the

Jim Carrey film *Bruce Almighty* (2003). In this zippier sequel, local Buffalo TV newsman Evan Baxter (Steve Carell) gets elected to Congress and packs up the family to move to suburban northern Virginia. On arriving at his new post, strange and comical things start happening. Soon God himself (Morgan Freeman) appears to Evan and commands him to build an ark because—naturally—a flood is coming.

Evan's family suspects that he is having a midlife crisis, and as his behavior grows ever odder, his wife, Joan (Lauren Graham), and his three sons eventually leave for her mother's house, abandoning him to build the ark himself. Yet weeks after Joan leaves Evan, in one of the more poignant scenes of the movie, God—disguised as a waiter in a diner—appears to Evan's mistrusting wife. He offers some worthy advice, surprisingly orthodox for Hollywood's new age armchair theologians. He tells her that God doesn't always give things; he gives the opportunity to get things. Here's how the scene plays out—God says:

> Let me ask you something. If someone prays for patience, you think God gives them patience? Or does he give them the opportunity to be patient? If he prayed for courage, does God give him courage, or does he give him opportunities to be courageous? If someone prayed for the family to be closer, do you think God zaps them with warm fuzzy feelings, or does he give them opportunities to love each other?

Getting the point, Joan rejoins Evan to finish the ark together. They work as a family, and God makes wonderful things happen. Despite its silliness, this film underscores the need to cooperate with God's grace. He respects our free will and does not force us—but rather enables us—to become virtuous.

So what are the occasions God gives us to become more trusting? What role are we to play in this process?

CHOOSING TO TRUST

We have seen that what comes naturally to children must often be relearned by adults, which begs the question: Can trust really be learned?

Isn't it the case that we either have it or we don't? We have to remember that trust involves *choice*. Moreover, trust in God is not a onetime affair or a single act; it is a virtue, a *good habit*. Habits are patterns of behavior that have become spontaneous or second nature to us. Some habits come naturally, but most of them are learned. This is really good news for all of us who realize that we aren't everything we should be. There is hope! Just because I have trouble trusting now doesn't mean I can never learn!

How are habits acquired? They are formed by a *repetition of actions*. You could try this little experiment. Over the period of a month, every time you serve yourself a drink out of a bottle or carton, always pour with your left hand. Every time you need to pour yourself or someone else a drink, consciously do so with *that* hand. If you start to take the bottle or carton with your right hand, move it to your left before pouring. At the end of the month, stop thinking about it. You will find that you now *spontaneously* pour always with your left hand! You have formed a habit.

This is true in just about every aspect of our lives. Surely you already have dozens of habits you aren't even fully aware of. Start paying attention to the way you do things, your little morning and evening rituals. You will find that you do most things the same way, day in and day out. They are routine for you, a *habitual* way of being and acting! You could change most of these if you wanted to, just by consciously doing things differently for a sustained period of time. Depending on how ingrained your present habits are, you will need more or less time to form new habits to replace them.

I think you can see where I am going with this. The habit or virtue of trust is formed by many repeated acts of trust. By *choosing* to trust again and again, you gradually form the virtue of trust. If we want to become trusting, we need to perform acts of trust in the here and now, knowing that little by little trust will become an ingrained habit.

EXERCISES TO BUILD TRUST

Believe it or not, on the Internet there are entire Web sites dedicated to exercises for building trust. Most of these are secular, of course. They

aren't concerned so much with building trust in God as they are with creating a trusting atmosphere in a work or school setting. One Web site, for
instance, advertises that "trust building activities help people to develop
mutual respect, openness, understanding, and empathy, as well as helping
to develop communication and teamwork skills."[1] Teamwork depends on
trust. Yet despite this notable difference, these exercises can shed much
light on what it means to trust in God as well.

One of the most typical of these activities is called the Trust Fall,
which I described earlier. It involves a person falling backward from table
height into the arms and hands of the group. The way the activity is generally set up, each member takes a turn as "faller" and the rest of the time
participates as a "catcher." The "faller" stands on a flat surface of table
height, crosses his arms across his chest, closes his eyes, and falls straight
backward into the waiting arms of the group. The idea is that the faller
should do so in as relaxed and trusting a way as possible, without buckling
or stiffening.

The aim of this activity is to learn to place one's trust completely in others, knowing that they won't let you down. Normally we like to see where we
are going and to take the necessary precautions not to hurt ourselves. In this
exercise, the "precaution" is simply to put one's confidence in others.

Another trust-building activity goes by the name of Minefield. In this
exercise, objects are scattered in an indoor or outdoor place. In pairs, one
person verbally guides his or her partner through the minefield. One person is blindfolded and cannot talk. The guide can see and talk but cannot
enter the field or touch the person. The challenge is for each blindfolded
person to walk from one side of the field to the other, avoiding the "mines"
by listening to the verbal instructions of his or her partner. This exercise
can be adapted to youth or adults and seeks to build both trust and communication skills.

Other trust-building activities include "Willow in the Wind," "Trust
Lean," "Running Free," "Slice 'n' Dice," and "Leap of Faith." All start with
the premise that trust is difficult, and that we need to learn to overcome
our natural desire to be in control of our own fate. Believing in other
people means a willingness to place one's well-being in their care.

Building trust in God obviously involves a different sort of activity. It would be silly to play "Leap of Faith" with God, throwing ourselves off a cliff and then shouting out, "God, catch me!" This would be similar to the devil's taunting Jesus to throw himself off the temple, relying on God's angels to catch him (see Luke 4:9–12). As we have seen, we don't grow in trust by *testing* God but by doing things his way, with the confidence that they will turn out well.

God himself gives us many opportunities to grow in trust. We don't need to invent them; we simply need to recognize them and take advantage of them. He is the one who provides the "exercises" we need to increase our confidence in him.

TRUST AND MEMORY

Of all the possible exercises we have to build trust, perhaps the most effective—and the most biblical—is the exercise of memory. To bolster our trust, God asks us to *remember*. He treats us the way he treated the Israelites. He often began his discourses to them by recalling his providential care for them and his feats of power in their midst. How often do we read, "I am the LORD your God, who brought you out of the land of Egypt"? In other words, "If I could handle your slavery in Egypt, don't you think I am able to resolve your lesser problems now?" And God encourages them, commands them to remember.

Thus Moses says to the people: "Remember this day on which you came out of Egypt, out of the house of slavery, because the LORD brought you out from there by strength of hand" (Exod. 13:3). Memorials are set up; reminders are worn on the forehead and the tassels of one's garments; children are brought up to recall God's portents in their favor. Why all of this remembering? Why these memorials? Because to remember the past is to trust in the future. To recall God's faithfulness is to recognize that he *was and is* faithful, then and now.

Paul teaches us how to invoke memory in our own lives, to draw strength from the experience of God's faithful love:

We do not want you to be unaware, brothers and sisters, of the afflic-
tion we experienced in Asia; for we were so utterly, unbearably crushed
that we despaired of life itself. Indeed, we felt that we had received the
sentence of death so that we would rely not on ourselves but on God
who raises the dead. *He who rescued us from so deadly a peril will continue
to rescue us*; on him we have set our hope that he will rescue us again.
(2 Corinthians 1:8–10, emphasis added)

Paul's memory of God's past trustworthiness is his greatest assurance
that God will continue to be faithful in the future. It is the awareness of
those past experiences that allows Paul to trust now, in the present moment.
Yet memory isn't the only way to build trust in God either. There are moments in life that are especially favorable to practicing trust and that enable
us to become more trusting over time. Let's examine these for a moment.

SCHOOLS OF TRUST

When people really want to learn something, they go to school. Nowadays
there are schools for everything. Think of kids who are serious about athlet-
ics and want to be the best. There are basketball camps, soccer camps, tennis camps, and football camps. For languages, too, school is a must. Students
coming to Rome often enroll in intensive Italian courses, which allows them to
quickly get up to speed to function in a new environment. People who want to
learn to draw or paint often sign up for art school, and so on in nearly every
field. These schools provide training, content, supervision, and important feed-
back to know how we are doing and correct errors before they go too far.

What about a virtue like trust? Wouldn't it be nice if there was a school to
learn to practice trust the way we would like to? Fortunately, there are several!

PRAYER

To regain or grow our trust, the first thing we need to do is *pray*. Of
all the things we pray for, increased trust should be near the top of the
list. Jesus taught us to place our needs before God, to ask that we might

receive (see Luke 11:9), and we all need trust. He can heal our wounded hearts and allow us a peace that we can find nowhere else. He can repair our inabilities to trust and calm our doubts and fears. The paradoxical thing is that our prayer for trust is at the same time an *exercise* in trust. We wouldn't pray, after all, if we didn't trust at all. Maybe when we pray for trust we are like the man in the Bible whose son suffered from the presence of an unclean spirit. He says to Jesus, "I believe; help my unbelief!" (Mark 9:24). In other words, he already did believe, but he knew that he could and should believe more. In the same way, when we pray we are already trusting, while at the same time asking for more trust.

Prayer is a refuge when everything else is against us. When all our friends have left us, in prayer we find God patiently expecting us. When our projects have failed and it seems our entire lives are falling apart, God is waiting for us, a good and faithful friend. When no one else has time for me, God still has time. When no one else listens anymore, God still listens. When everyone else has given up on me, God hasn't. When it seems as if there is no solution to my problems, God becomes my solution.

In prayer, together with God, we learn to see things as they really are. We see how many things we once trusted in were unworthy of our trust. We realize that few things in life truly matter, and that we expend far too much time and energy chasing after things that will never fill us. As Pope Benedict has written,

> To pray is not to step outside history and withdraw to our own private corner of happiness. When we pray properly we undergo a process of inner purification that opens us up to God and thus to our fellow human beings as well. In prayer we must learn what we can truly ask of God—what is worthy of God. We must learn that we cannot pray against others. We must learn that we cannot ask for the superficial and comfortable things that we desire at this moment—that meagre, misplaced hope that leads us away from God. We must learn to purify our desires and our hopes. We must free ourselves from the hidden lies with which we deceive ourselves. God sees through them, and when we come before God, we too are forced to recognize them.[2]

In this way prayer provides a much-needed purification of our hopes and aspirations. Placing ourselves in God's presence in prayer is like standing before a mirror that shows only the truth, and from whose gaze nothing escapes. He reveals what is best and worst in us, and we are moved to pray with the psalmist: "Who can detect their errors? Clear me from hidden faults" (Ps. 19:12). Yet, in prayer, Jesus gently teaches us to find in him not only the truth, but also the way and the life. That is, as real as our faults may be, he always has the cure. His love and grace give us the courage to accept the truth, to unveil ourselves as we are, shunning the refuge of deceit. Our trust in him emboldens us to embrace the challenge of our Christian lives with no shortcuts or subterfuges.

Prayer also allows us to exercise our memories together with God, like two friends fondly recalling their past escapades together. In prayer we reminisce with God about our experiences together, and we cannot help realizing that through thick and thin he has been by our side. Even when things seemed darkest, he was there.

THE APOSTOLATE

Our endeavors to extend Christ's kingdom provide another key school of trust in God. When we take on projects for God, we recognize more clearly our need for him. We realize right off the bat that "unless the LORD builds the house, those who build it labor in vain. Unless the LORD guards the city, the guard keeps watch in vain" (Ps. 127:1). Divine projects demand divine assistance. Only he can make our work truly fruitful in a lasting, meaningful way.

Working for Christ's kingdom also helps us overcome the ambivalence of wondering, especially when our efforts revolve around our own career advancement, whether what we are doing is really God's will. As

I really had no idea what trust was until I started teaching Sunday school! Even though the kids I was teaching were pretty good, I was terrified. All I could do was commend myself to the Lord's care and throw myself into the work. By recognizing my own incompetence, I had no choice but to lean on him all the more. I think I got more out of that experience than my students did!

—JACKIE, AGE 20

long as this ambivalence remains, our trust can waver, too, since we don't know whether we are working for ourselves or for him. When we place ourselves at the service of Christ and his Church, however, this doubt disappears. We know that he will bless our efforts in the best way possible. The outcome may not match what we had foreseen, but we know that it will be fruitful nonetheless, and more fruitful than we imagined.

God often asks us to do things that vastly surpass our possibilities. In this way he stretches our trust, asking us to rely more on him than on our own talents and abilities. By pushing us out of our comfort zone, he makes trust a necessity. It was not David's skill with a sling that allowed him to kill the giant Goliath. It was not Peter's brilliance or leadership qualities that allowed him to determinedly guide Christ's young Church after Pentecost. It was not Paul's rhetorical prowess that made him such a successful apostle to the Gentiles. As soon as we perceive Christ's call, we must perform an act of trust. We go out on a limb for him. We know that if he calls, he must also furnish all the necessary tools we need to complete the task he asks of us. Even little setbacks will not discourage a Christian who has heard God's call and tries to fulfill it with trust and purity of heart. In this way we truly become God's coworkers, contributing to the salvation of the world.

TRIALS AND SUFFERING

We should practice trust always, in good times and bad. God is always there with us. As the psalmist says, "If I go up to heaven, you are there; if I go down to the grave, you are there" (Ps. 139:8 NLT). In good times, we gather strength and trust for the more difficult moments. But as helpful as this is, without a doubt our trust grows most when it is tried.

Just as an athlete makes most progress when facing a tough opponent, our trust makes great strides when it is tested. I remember when I used to play tennis a lot I would make my greatest leaps forward when I had to take on someone better than myself. It was a scary thing, and often I preferred to play people whose skill was at the same level or worse than my own. It is a very daunting enterprise to stand up to an adversary who is more experienced or powerful than you are. Yet these were my best games. These were the games in which I could literally feel my strokes improving, where I had to give my utmost just to survive. And the funny thing is, after that contest the improvement stayed with me. I was a better player from that moment on.

What is true of trials and opposition is also true of sorrow and suffering. When we suffer, we realize how frail we are and how little it takes to incapacitate us. When I have a splitting headache or a sprained ankle (to take the tiniest examples!), I suddenly find myself unable to do many things I ordinarily take for granted. My usual rhythm is knocked out of whack. I feel as if I have been defeated, or at least greatly impeded, by something insignificant. But these sufferings, little or great, make us realize how very fragile we are. They make us turn to the one who is the true source of our strength and effectiveness. When we are healthy and everything is hunky-dory, we can feel powerful, even invincible. Suffering brings us back to reality and invites us to turn back to God.

In these occasions, we also have the opportunity to practice a simple but ancient tradition, that of "offering up" our sufferings to God. Our sufferings acquire value and meaning when we unite them with the sufferings of Christ. This is not just some pious fiction but expresses the Christian understanding that when Jesus united himself to our humanity, he united each one of us to himself. The little annoyances that dot our days become precious occasions to give something back to God, asking him

Putting trust in God means having faith that God knows what is best for us better than we do; that He has a plan of which we can only see small pieces that don't seem to make sense on their own. Trusting Him means that despite the confusion when confronted with the small pieces, we have faith that there is that bigger picture, that bigger plan. I think trust in God manifests itself as an inward peace— peace of mind knowing that God loves us, has a plan for us, and will provide us with what we need. I know some argue that the suffering in the world is proof that God is not trustworthy: "How can we say we can trust God to provide when people are starving to death? He clearly didn't provide for them." That seems a rather small understanding of the providence of God. Perhaps the suffering He allows us to endure is what we need to grow closer to Him, which is far more important that sustaining our earthly lives.

—KATIE, AGE 24

to bless them and make them fruitful for ourselves and others. Our trust in God's ability to bring good out of evil transforms our daily aches and bothers into something of eternal significance.

Suffering schools us in trust in another way as well. Sometimes nothing seems to relieve the pain. Some pains—like a broken heart—can seem to be terminal, incurable, and fatal. People can bring us Tylenol and ibuprofen. They can drug us with morphine or try to distract us with chitchat. In the end, our pain is deeper than that. There are some wounds that only God can heal, some sorrows that only God can understand and eventually relieve. Sorrow easily makes us realize how weak human remedies are and can teach us to trust in God alone.

If this is true of the sorrows of which we are the victims, it is also true of sorrows of which we are the cause. How can we right the wrongs we have done? How can we make up for the pain that we have caused others? How can we rectify the stupid, selfish choices we have made? This, too, is a school of trust. We learn to look to God to make up for our mistakes. We need him to heal and forgive us. We also need him to make right what we have made wrong. We can say we're sorry. We can try to make amends. But only God can truly set right what sin has broken. We must trust in him rather than ourselves.

Whether we have caused them or not, witnessing others' sorrows easily brings a feeling of powerlessness. We would like to help. We would like to say something, do something, to make everything all right. And we cannot. We either anguish in despair or turn to the one who *can* do something. And here the greatest gift we can give the loved one who suffers is a share in our own trust. When we truly believe, we are able to offer hope. If our own trust is weak, we have nothing to offer. When we are convinced that everything, even suffering, has meaning and value in God, and that he will one day make all things right, we can offer hope and even the prospect of joy.

JUDGMENT

Another school of trust comes from somewhere we might not expect— the idea of Last Judgment. From the beginning of recorded history, humanity has found death to be the biggest enigma of our earthly existence.

It just doesn't make sense. Man's spirit cries out for immortality, and we cannot accept the notion that this short life is all there is. In fact, a refusal to accept the idea that we simply "cease to be" has kept people hoping that death does not have the final word. Some have turned to a belief in reincarnation, others to a belief in historical recurrence, still others to a belief in passage to a higher existence.

The Christian response to this is summed up in the "eternal truths" or the "last things" (in Greek, *eschata*), which include death, judgment, heaven, and hell. We believe not only that death does not mean the end of our existence, but that it marks the beginning of our true lives together with God in eternity. It is not the end, but a passage, after which comes resurrection. Yet this passage also includes a rendering of accounts to God our Creator, where we will be judged on the way we used our freedom while on earth. Our thoughts, words, deeds, and omissions—our response to God's grace in our lives—will be the matter for this final exam. As John of the Cross famously put it, "At the evening of life, we shall be judged on our love."[3]

The thought of judgment serves as an incentive for our good actions and a deterrent to sin, but it also serves as a stimulus for *trust*. As we recall that the one who will judge us, Jesus Christ, is also our Savior and Redeemer, we exercise our trust in his mercy. Who could stand before God on his own merits? Who would dare to claim a "right" to enter heaven, if not for the salvation that Christ won for us? As Jesus said, "Be alert at all times, praying that you may have the strength to escape all these things that will take place, and to stand before the Son of Man" (Luke 21:36). We all have need of God's mercy, and without it, none of us can appear before his judgment seat. But the one who will judge is Love himself, who ardently desires our union with him. As the apostle Paul reminds us, God "desires everyone to be saved and to come to the knowledge of the truth" (1 Tim. 2:4). This knowledge of God's saving grace will inspires us to trust in him and to turn to him in hope.

In looking to judgment, we also trust in eternal justice. All the unfairness that fills our world, making us cry out for the plight of the innocent and the apparent impunity of the wicked, finds its resolution in God's final reckoning of the world. Everything that didn't make sense in this world will finally receive an answer in the world to come. We will look on human history in a completely new light, understanding God's providence and wisdom and praising him for his goodness. In trust we look forward to that day, and this trust permits us to bear patiently the uncertainties and confusion of the present age. We believe that in the final hour, there will be "an 'undoing' of past suffering, a reparation that sets things aright."[4] Only God can rectify the historical injustices that throw the harmony of our world on its head.

In the end, the image of the Last Judgment is an image of hope and trust rather than terror and despair. We look in hopeful expectation for the coming of Christ, who will put all things right. Our faith gives us an assurance of judgment that fills us with peace in the turbulence of our lives, and a hope not only for ourselves, but for all who have sought truth and goodness, and for all who have suffered. It is to that day we look with trust and confidence—when "God will wipe every tear from their eyes" (Rev. 7:17 NLT).

As is the case with any school, there are good students and bad students. Good schools do not guarantee a perfect outcome. Personal effort and application are required. For some, personal suffering produces only complaints and lamentations, rather than an increased trust in God. For some, prayer consists of a thoughtless repetition of words, rather than an intimate encounter with the one in whom we have placed our trust. For some, the thought of judgment provokes only fear and trembling, rather than a gentle assurance of God's final victory. Yet for those good students who use these schools well, a sterling opportunity is offered to forge a deeper trust in God day by day. This confidence can become the rock-solid foundation upon which are built lives of holiness and peace.

Another key element to growth in trust remains. It is the choice to leave aside other options. A boundless trust in God cannot coexist with other safety nets. But does God really mean for us to abandon all other possible securities? Let's look more closely.

17

BECOMING POOR
IN SPIRIT

You have probably heard the story—a favorite for preachers—of the man who falls over the edge of a cliff and barely survives by grasping a branch on the way down. Suspended over a dizzying drop-off, the man desperately cries out for help. "Is there anybody up there?" he shouts. And again, "I said, is there anybody up there?" After some minutes, the man is astonished to hear a response, a thunderous voice from above that says, "I am God." The man quickly responds, "That is wonderful! What good fortune. Please, can you get me safely down from here?" God replies, "Of course I can." "What should I do?" the man asks. And God answers, "Just let go of the branch and I will catch you." Dead silence follows. Surveying his situation again, the man pauses, then shouts upward, "Is there anybody *else* up there?"

The punch line of this story illustrates an important truth. We don't so much mind trusting in God as we mind letting go of everything else. Only inveterate gamblers are willing to let go of a sure thing for the remote possibility of greater gains, and a sure branch may seem more reliable than God's promise to catch us when we fall. Yet trusting in someone often means letting go of something else. Sometimes we must let go of one handhold—which has supported us until now—in order to seize a new, more secure handhold that God is offering us. We cannot continue hanging on to both at the same time. Similarly, you can tell whether the ice on a pond will hold you up only when you have put your weight on it. You can tell that God is trustworthy only when you have leaned on him.

TRUST AND SPIRITUAL POVERTY

The virtue of confidence in God demands real "poverty of spirit," a willingness to let go of other handrails and abandon ourselves totally to him. Other securities not only don't help us trust in God, they can even be a hindrance. Sometimes only by leaving them by the wayside do we realize how strong we are with God's grace.

Think again of the story of David and Goliath. We all know the basics of the story of how the little guy defeats the Philistine giant with nothing but a sling and a few rocks. But there is an important detail of this encounter that we shouldn't forget. Sent out to face the Philistine, David is clad in Saul's heavy armor, which is supposed to provide him with the best possible protection against the heavy odds he faces. And yet David finds himself encumbered rather than aided by the armor, and he can barely walk or lift his arms. What seemed to be protection was really an impediment. So in the end David lays the armor aside, defenseless except for his absolute trust in the Lord. And he *wins*.

Saul's armor could easily represent for us all the human qualities and abilities we are tempted to rely on in life. Our street smarts, our contacts and networking, our bank accounts and investment portfolios, our rhetoric and powers of persuasion, our experience and know-how—none of these will save us in the end. None will guarantee us victory where it really counts, and none will make us spiritually fruitful. The evangelical virtue of "poverty of spirit" means a stubborn unwillingness to place our trust anywhere but in God.

Christ does not want to be our last resort when all else fails. He wants to be our first and absolute source of strength and confident assurance. He wants us to proclaim, together with the apostle Paul, "I can do all things through him who strengthens me" (Phil. 4:13). Confidence in Christ does not mean we will not have difficulties, but that he will give us the grace to overcome them and will accompany us in the struggle every step of the way. He will never leave us alone. Christ assured his disciples at the

Last Supper: "In the world you face persecution. But take courage; I have conquered the world" (John 16:33). In fact, Jesus repeats his command of "take courage" or "fear not" again and again to his followers. He seems to be telling us, "How can you be afraid when I am with you?"

Trust, we have said, is the necessary complement to humility. A healthy distrust of self is compensated by a well-founded trust in God. We can afford to lower our guard only when we are sure that someone else is watching our backs. Often we cling to our independence because we fear we can depend on only ourselves. We think self-reliance is our only option and no one else deserves our trust. Maybe we have been let down. Maybe we have been burned one too many times. But the one who never burns us is God. He may not guarantee us a Sunday picnic, but he will stand by our side in good times and in bad, giving us the grace and strength we need.

BUYING AND SELLING

Another biblical teaching can make this clearer still. Jesus taught that the kingdom of heaven is like a treasure buried in a field. When a man stumbles upon the treasure he knows he must do anything he can to possess it. Maybe you can picture the scene at the beginning of the old *Beverly Hillbillies* TV series where Jed Clampett is hunting and his gunshot sets oil gushing out of the ground. He can't believe his good fortune. This was what it was like for the man in Jesus' parable who discovers the buried treasure; he is absolutely thrilled! So the man goes home, *sells everything he owns*, and buys the field—along with the treasure in it! (See Matt. 13:44.) He has made the deal of his life. He doesn't care that he has sold his home, with his refrigerator, stereo and worn-out armchair. He has gotten something infinitely more valuable in its place!

Jesus tells another parable just like it, where a merchant in search of fine pearls finds one stunning pearl of immense value. Thrilled, he *sells everything he owns* and buys it. It is everything he has ever wanted and caps his years of commerce in pearls. The search is over, since he has found what his heart desired. (See Matt. 13:45.)

As you can see, the common thread running through both parables involves finding, selling, and buying. Some things are worth so much, the only way to own them is to sell everything else we have. How else are we to buy them? Sometimes we have to abandon all to possess all, empty ourselves in order to be filled, sell all in order to own all. If we are going to lean on God and trust in him fully, we need to take our weight off our other securities. In the end we can put our weight on only one support. We need to make the personal decision of where we will step. Which hand-hold or foothold guarantees the security I am looking for?

In the Scriptures, Jesus often speaks of necessary choices between in-compatible things. He discourages trying to have our cake and eat it, too. For instance, he tells his followers that they must choose whom they will serve: God or money (see Luke 16:13). His teaching seems very severe: "No one can serve two masters; for a slave will either hate the one and love the other, or be devoted to the one and despise the other" (Matt. 6:24). In this context, "serving" means more than ministering to, attending to, or taking care of. In the ancient world, a master was both lord and protector; a servant gave his allegiance and labor and received defense and refuge. It was a two-way street. When a person attached himself to a master like this, he became his servant, but he also gained personal security. Here, "serving" also resembles trusting, since the one we serve is also our provider and de-fender. To serve here means to live for, to pursue with dedication, to look to for guidance and security. We can put our full interest in only one thing. We can expect happiness from only one source. We must likewise choose whom we will trust. Taking Jesus as Lord and Master means both serving him and trusting in him alone.

Jesus himself was very tough in express-ing the need to trust in him alone. He uses a radical expression: no one can come to Christ without "hating" mother and father, wife, children, and even his own life (see Luke 14:26). These are all competitors, not only for the love that belongs to God alone, but also for his trust. They all must take second place to the trust that we owe to God.

> *I kind of trust God, but I don't only trust God, you know? I mean, you have to trust other things, too, right? Sometimes God helps you but sometimes he doesn't. You need other options. I trust God but I think I trust myself more.*
>
> —Dan, age 25

STRIPPING THE APOSTLES

There is something truly strange about the way Christ sends out the twelve apostles, and later about the way he sends the seventy-two disciples. You remember these scenes. Jesus sends out the disciples in pairs to every town and place that he intends to visit, to prepare the way. Yet rather than *equip* them, he *strips* them. Rather than offer a series of helpful tools, he takes away the few tools that they have. Rather than arm them, he disarms them. He wants them to feel needy and naked. Here is what Jesus commands the apostles: "You received without payment; give without payment. Take no gold, or silver, or copper in your belts, no bag for your journey, or two tunics, or sandals, or a staff; for laborers deserve their food" (Matt. 10:8–10).

To the seventy-two, Jesus says something very similar:

> Go on your way. See, I am sending you out like lambs into the midst of wolves. Carry no purse, no bag, no sandals; and greet no one on the road. Whatever house you enter, first say, "Peace to this house!" And if anyone is there who shares in peace, your peace will rest on that person; but if not, it will return to you. (Luke 10:3–6)

Hmmmm. This doesn't exactly read like a recipe for success. Not only does Jesus not offer subsidies for a successful journey, he takes away the little they have! If you or I were to offer a list of recommendations for people taking a journey, it surely wouldn't look like this. We would remind our friends to take along a toothbrush, pajamas, a change of underwear, a sweater and a light jacket (in case it gets cold), a cell phone and a directory of important phone numbers, some emergency money, and dozens of other things that could be useful "just in case." Jesus doesn't do that. He presents not a list of the things they will need to take along, but a list of the things they *won't* need! *Don't take money. Don't take an extra suitcase. Don't take sandals. Don't take a walking staff.* . . . What is Jesus doing here?

He is teaching us about *spiritual poverty*. He is teaching his followers what it means—in practice, and not just in theory—to be poor in spirit. This isn't a poverty imposed by circumstance, but an evangelical poverty intentionally sought and freely practiced. He is asking us to *choose* to be poor. But why would we want to practice this sort of poverty? Why would Jesus request it? Because it obliges us to trust more in God and less in human securities. How many times Jesus warns his followers of the danger of riches! How often he cautions us about putting our security in anything other than his grace! As Jesus said to Paul when Paul was feeling especially needful and deprived of support: "My grace is sufficient for you" (2 Cor. 12:9).

Do you think Jesus' admonitions against the perils of riches have to do with a hatred of money or success? Do you think Jesus thought gold was evil or that silver rotted the soul? Of course not! All of creation is good. Every created thing bears the imprint of its Maker and testifies to his goodness and providence. Jesus never asks us to despise his Father's work. The problem with riches is not that BMWs and swimming pools and Spanish villas and vacations and stock portfolios are evil, but that when we possess many things, we are tempted to *rely* on them. We are tempted to see in them the source of our safety and well-being. In short, they can compete with the security that we are meant to find in God *alone*.

SPRING CLEANING

So what does this mean for us, practically? What consequences should this have in the life of a twenty-first-century man or woman? Should you pitch the sofa out the window and clear all the designer dresses and shoes out of your closet to take to the nearest homeless shelter? Not necessarily. Spiritual poverty is above all a disposition of the heart. It means an inner *attachment* to God and *detachment* from everything that is not God, along with a willingness to sacrifice everything for God if it comes down to that.

But even though spiritual poverty is above all an inner disposition, it also has real consequences for our lives. We show whether we are poor in spirit when we have to make choices. When we pay more attention to a money-making deal than to a neighbor in distress, when we read the *Wall Street Journal* more devoutly than we read God's Word, when we weep more over a drop in the price of IBM stock than we do over a friend who has lost her faith in God, then we know we are definitely not poor in spirit. Spiritual poverty shows itself in our priorities, in our values, and in our daily decisions.

The sort of poverty that Jesus asks of us is not a punishment; it is a gift. It does not bind us; it frees us. It allows us to walk through this world as pilgrims who know that our homeland and our hearts are elsewhere. Spiritual poverty keeps us from becoming unduly euphoric over our worldly gains or unduly distraught over our worldly losses.

Jesus promised that the truth—his truth—would set us free (see John 8:32). A true Christian is liberated from the unbearable weight of earthly anxiety. Our faith enables us to takes the capricious shifts of fortune in stride, neither rejoicing too much over what has little eternal value nor weeping too much when worldly treasures fail. Look how beautifully Paul expressed the freedom and peace of soul that this inner detachment brought:

> I have learned to be content with whatever I have. I know what it is to have little, and I know what it is to have plenty. In any and all circumstances I have learned the secret of being well-fed and of going hungry, of having plenty and of being in need. I can do all things through him who strengthens me. (Philippians 4:11–13)

Yet this inner freedom doesn't just happen; it is the fruit of real choices. We need to consciously opt for Christ and opt against dependence on the world. *Affective* poverty (poverty of the heart) needs to have an *effective* expression (poverty in practice). Sometimes we need to cut excess things out of our lives. Sometimes we need to simplify. In the same way a porn addict may need to get rid of his Internet connection because it is too much a temptation, we may need to clear out those things that clutter our relationship with God and threaten to take his place in our lives. This is true not only of sinful things, but of anything that binds or overly distracts us. Sometimes things that are not bad in themselves become bad for us when they become too important to us, when we feel as if we couldn't live without them. Don't you sometimes feel that you would be closer to God if you didn't have so many "things" crowding your life? Don't you sometimes wish you could clear out some of the worthless junk that accumulates in your heart, in order to love God with a greater singleness of purpose?

I often procrastinate in cleaning my office until I can't bear it anymore. I know it would be easier if I did it *every day* the way I should, so that things wouldn't build up, but I haven't yet formed this habit. Still, there is nothing like the feeling of finally going through so much stuff (*Where did I get this? What is this doing here? I don't need that!*) and getting rid of most of it. What freedom of spirit when I can finally clear out all the waste and return to a simpler, more spartan sort of existence. It reminds me of the desert, where, in the austerity of nature, the Spirit speaks with greater clarity.

IS GOD ENOUGH?

Perhaps the most radical example of this spiritual poverty comes from those Christians who receive the calling to give a special witness of God's greatness in their lives. Like the rich young man in the Gospel of Matthew, they are called literally to sell all, to give their money to the poor, and then to follow in Jesus' footsteps (see 19:21). By doing without things the world considers indispensable, consecrating themselves totally to God, they provide a dramatic testimony of the power of his love to fill the human heart. They preach the love of Christ as evangelizers to the world and ask for nothing in return except God himself. Where would the world be without the monks, nuns, and priests, the pastors and missionaries, who through the ages have given their lives to God alone? And Jesus promises wonderful things for those who abandon everything for him. He says, "Everyone who has left houses or brothers or sisters or father or mother or children or fields, for my name's sake, will receive a hundredfold, and will inherit eternal life" (Matt. 19:29). The greatest gift of all, though, is not the hundredfold that Jesus promises, but the gift of God himself.

Although not everyone is called to this level of evangelical poverty, all of us are called to clear our lives of useless distractions and frivolous pur-

> *I sometimes wish I could leave the world behind. I would like to make my trust in God more real, like a life choice rather than an insurance policy. Sometimes I think about it, but it's tough, you know? So I have never done it. Not yet.*
>
> —JOHN, AGE 28

suits. Why, after all, do Christians make sacrifices or offer acts of abnega-
tion? Why offer up a piece of chocolate cake or give up television for Lent?
What is the purpose of these centuries-old Christian practices?

They serve as a reminder. These practices test our resolve and put our
priorities back in place. They safeguard our poverty of spirit by allowing
us to do without certain unnecessary things from time to time. They testify to our commitment to love the Lord with our whole hearts and souls,
while being ready to do without other things. Jesus said that if something
is an obstacle to our relationship with him, we should simply get rid of it.
Nothing is worth losing God over. Jesus' exact words were these:

> If your hand causes you to stumble, cut it off; it is better for you to
> enter life maimed than to have two hands and to go to hell, to the un-
> quenchable fire. And if your foot causes you to stumble, cut it off; it is
> better for you to enter life lame than to have two feet and to be thrown
> into hell. And if your eye causes you to stumble, tear it out; it is better
> for you to enter the kingdom of God with one eye than to have two
> eyes and to be thrown into hell, where their worm never dies, and the
> fire is never quenched. (Mark 9:43–48)

In the end, by teaching us to be spiritually poor, Jesus teaches us to be
smart businessmen and businesswomen! *Don't throw away something of eternal
value for something of merely temporal value,* he tells us. *Learn how to distinguish what is
solid from what is flimsy.* Some things are temporary and some things are permanent; some things are passing and others are lasting and eternal. A Christian
is called to build his house on the solid rock of eternal things, rather than the
sandy foundations of passing things such as earthly wealth and success.

Christian poverty—lived as a virtue—is not merely the absence of superfluous things. Like all Christian virtues, it is not emptiness or a lack of anything. It
is a choice for God. We empty ourselves of worthless trifles to fill ourselves with
true riches. We store up riches in heaven, where they can never be lost, instead of
amassing riches on earth, where they must eventually come to naught (see Matt.
6:19–20). By renouncing the passing things that the world considers precious,
we are free to set our hearts on treasures of far greater value.

All through history the saints have had priorities that differed from the world's. They realized that what is truly worthwhile is that which brings us closer to God. In the BBC series *The Tudors*, the queen Catherine of Aragon, Henry VIII's first wife, says something beautiful in this regard. When she hears the painful news that Henry will be marrying Anne Boleyn, she says: "If I had to choose between extreme happiness and extreme sorrow, I would always choose sorrow. For when you are happy you forget about spiritual things; you forget about God. But in your sorrow, he is always with you." This logic makes no sense to those whose hearts are set on the pleasures of this world, but it makes perfect sense to those who wish to amass treasure in heaven.

Again, Jesus tells us these things not to make us sad but to make us happy, not to bring us down but to raise us up and give us lasting joy. Spiritual poverty was Christ's choice for himself. He was born in a stable, with no more royal court than some poor shepherds and animals. He lived free of attachments to material things, so much so that his very food was to do the will of his Father (see John 4:34). He had no place to call his own, nowhere even to lay his head (see Luke 9:58). He died poor, too, on a rough wooden cross, surrounded by thieves, and was eventually laid in a borrowed tomb (see Matt. 27:60). When we imitate Christ in his poverty, we also share in his peace. A Christian who lives with his treasure in heaven and his trust in God is spared the anxieties that this world often brings.

Of course, God does not intend for us to live irresponsibly. We are called to be good stewards of our talents, to responsibly care for those entrusted to us. We need to work, earn money, save, and prepare for the future. Yet, ultimately, we live with the firm conviction that we have here "no lasting city" (Heb. 13:14). The world and its treasures will not save us, nor will the lack of them destroy us. The world as we know it is "passing away" (1 Cor. 7:31).

Fortunately, to aid in our efforts to grow in spiritual poverty and to place our trust in God alone, he has given us a playbook. His Word is a light for our paths, and in the area of trust, the book of Psalms is particularly helpful. Let's take a look.

18

THE PSALMS:
A BOOK OF TRUST

Of all the means to grow in trust, two stand out as particularly successful. The first is the exercise of trust, whereby we act *as if* we trusted already. Many virtues grow fastest when we assume we already have them. A person who acts as if he is humble soon finds out—much to his surprise!—that he is, in fact, humble (or at least humbler than he was). The second means is prayer. This means both *asking* God for the trust we need and *offering* prayers of trust. Sometimes this means taking other people's words and making them our own.

Trust is a hallmark of the entire Christian Bible but perhaps is nowhere as evident as in the book of Psalms. The Psalms read like a litany of trust, or an antiphon of confidence in a God who never fails those who believe in him. For those who wish to grow in trust, there is no better playbook (or pray-book!) than the Psalms. It allows us both to exercise our trust and to ask for more. Praying the Psalms means acting as if we already possess the fullness of trust (though we may not feel it) and begging for more.

The Psalter was Israel's hymnbook or, to be more precise, the songbook of the temple. The book, often attributed at least in part to the authorship of King David, contains a collection of 150 psalms, which are sometimes divided into hymns of praise celebrating God's glory, psalms of suffering or laments, and psalms of thanksgiving. This three-way division is not absolute, and there is much overlap among the three types of Psalms. What is clear is that the theme of trust runs through all of them, like a common thread uniting the entire book.

The Psalms are true *prayers*. They are not just pious thoughts or reflections. They implore God in direct address, not just thinking about him, but also talking *to him*. So by reading the Psalms, we not only read, we pray. We use another's inspired words as the content for our prayer, but the prayer is truly ours. The Psalms teach us to pray as we ought.

Perhaps the most important thing we should have in mind when praying the Psalms is that they were *Jesus'* prayer book. This was his own manual of prayers, which he recited and relied on; the Psalms were Jesus' daily bread. When we pray the Psalms, we use the very prayers that Jesus used! We can almost hear him, glorifying his Father, begging assistance for his people, thanking God from the bottom of his heart for his infinite mercy and kindness. We use the exact same words he used, uniting ourselves to him in prayer to the Father.

Jesus often cited the Psalms from memory, showing how they referred to his mission and using their content for his own prayer. Quoting Psalm 118:22–23, Jesus observed: "The stone that the builders rejected has become the cornerstone; this was the Lord's doing, and it is amazing in our eyes" (Matt. 21:42). To show his preeminence over King David, Jesus cited Psalm 110:1, saying, " 'The Lord said to my Lord, "Sit at my right hand, until I make your enemies your footstool." ' David thus calls him 'Lord'; so how can he be his son?" (Luke 20:42–44). From the cross, Jesus intoned two psalms, making them his own prayer. First, in Matthew's Gospel, we find his anguished cry of abandonment, citing the first line of Psalm 22. "About the ninth hour Jesus cried with a loud voice, 'Eli, Eli, lama sabachthani?' that is, 'My God, my God, why have you forsaken me?' " (Matt. 27:46). Using the psalmist's words, Jesus expresses his feelings of solitude and loneliness. Instead of turning in on himself or looking elsewhere for consolation, he invokes the one who is always faithful. And as this beautiful and trusting psalm continues, it ends not in despair, but in a prayer praising God's never-failing love.

Just before dying, Jesus makes an explicit act of trust in God, citing

Psalm 31:5: "Into your hands I commend my spirit" (Luke 23:46). He entrusts his spirit, as he has entrusted his entire life, to his good and loving Father. But here Jesus deviates slightly from the original text, adding a single word, a word that only he could utter as the only begotten Son: *Abba! Father!* "Jesus, crying with a loud voice, said, '*Father*, into your hands I commit my spirit!' And having said this he breathed his last" (Luke 23:46, emphasis added). Up to the end, Jesus knew he was God's Son, and he spoke to his Father with the confidence that only a trusting child could have.

Jesus is in the Psalms, too, of course. The Psalms foretold the coming Messiah and gave the Israelites precious information of what to expect. They speak of him as an ideal man (see Ps. 1), as a king (see Pss. 2; 72), as a suffering savior (see Ps. 22), as a royal bridegroom (see Ps. 45), and as our high priest–king (see Ps. 110). So when he prayed the Psalms, Jesus found much food for reflection regarding his own identity and mission. But he also prayed as a faithful Israelite, meditating on the history of his people and on God's faithfulness all along the way.

Although the idea of trust is central to the entire Psalter, this doesn't mean just any kind of trust. The psalmist specifically advocates *trust in God*, rather than trust in any other possible source of security. The Psalms make the case that ultimately only the Lord is worthy of our absolute and unbounded trust. Nothing and no one else is.

CHOOSING RIGHTLY

Much of the psalmists' message revolves around the central theme of *choice*, specifically the choice of whom we shall serve, and in whom we shall place our trust. Whom shall we accept as God? Whom shall we worship? Whom shall we adore? To whom shall we turn for refuge, consolation, and salvation? This choice reveals itself most radically as an option between the one true God and false idols. Remember that choosing one's "god" meant more than choosing the object of one's worship. Just as important, it involved choosing one's protector. Let's look at how the psalmists compare the one true God with false idols.

The futility of trusting in these so-called gods is underscored by re-minding readers what they are made of. "The idols of the nations are silver and gold, the work of human hands. . . . Those who make them and all who trust them shall become like them" (Ps. 135:15, 18). What do these idols deliver? What can they promise? Nothing at all. Trusting in human handiwork leaves us building on sand, and our structure will soon be swept away. Yet the psalmist writes, "You hate those who pay regard to worthless idols, but I trust in the LORD" (Ps. 31:6). Here the author is aware that trusting in idols is not only a *fruitless* enterprise; it is also *displeasing* to God, who alone is worthy of trust.

On the other hand, the psalmist asks God to reward him for his un-swerving trust. "Vindicate me, O LORD," he says, "for I have walked in my integrity, and I have trusted in the LORD without wavering" (Ps. 26:1). In other words, by praying these words we remind God of his promises and ask him to uphold our cause. It is right to expect that God will repay those who trust in him by showing himself supremely worthy of that trust. He will deliver all they expect and even more.

This choice for God means finding in him our fortress, our rock and our protection. Look again at how the psalmist expresses this confidence:

> You, O Lord, are my hope,
>   my trust, O LORD, from my youth.
> Upon you I have leaned from my birth;
>   it was you who took me from my mother's womb.
> My praise is continually of you.
> I have been like a portent to many,
>   but you are my strong refuge.
>
> (Psalm 71:5–7)

Unlike false gods that can provide no protection and no sure defense, the Lord is true to his word and worthy of all our trust. Yet the psalmists don't merely speak about idols in an abstract way. They also get down to the nitty-gritty of very specific "idols" in which we might be tempted to place our trust. One of these idols refers to the "flesh."

GOD OR "FLESH"?

We all trust other people, especially people who love us and care for us, and we are right to do so. But the psalmists remind us that human beings, as good as they may be, can never provide the sure and lasting support we need. Other people are mere mortals like ourselves, and they are subject to all the limitations that we are.

Sometimes people's goodwill fails, and selfishness takes over. Human beings are notoriously changeable and fickle, and despite a thousand promises, they still fail. Other times people may have the best of intentions but are simply *unable* to help us. For example, when we are deathly sick, others may comfort us with their attention and love, but they *cannot* heal our ills, strengthen our spirits, or change our hearts. The psalmist draws together the many obstacles we face in life as "our foes," and writes: "O grant us help against the foe, for human help is worthless. With God we shall do valiantly; it is he who will tread down our foes" (Ps. 108:12–13). Sometimes our foes are external, like those who plot against us, betray us, or stab us in the back. Many other times our foes are internal, such as our own vices and temptations, or the difficulties we face in our relationships, employment, or personal lives. Against these, God provides us with strength of soul, so that "we shall do valiantly." When we are up against foes that we cannot defeat, he himself treads them down.

The psalmist says even more explicitly:

> *I really learned to trust in God when he helped me quit smoking. I had tried several times and always gave in. In the end I thought it was impossible, but I put everything in his hands and gave it another shot. Somehow he made it happen. It was impossible for me, but not for him.*
>
> —SUSAN, AGE 39

> Do not put your trust in princes,
>   in mortals, in whom there is no help.
> When their breath departs, they return to the earth;
>   on that very day their plans perish.

Happy are those whose help is the God of Jacob,
     whose hope is in the LORD their God,
who made heaven and earth,
     the sea, and all that is in them;
who keeps faith forever.

(Psalm 146:3–6)

Sometimes we are tempted to think that the solution to the world's problems is in better politics or in social programs. While these can indeed help, they do not give humanity what it ultimately needs. God alone gives that.

With his characteristic wisdom, the psalmist notes that princes are limited the same way you and I are. Both they and we "return to the earth" and often our "plans perish," despite our good intentions. It is God alone who never fails, and whose plans always succeed. He made heaven and earth and all that is in them. He is Lord of all. Moreover, the Lord "keeps faith forever." He doesn't say one thing one day, then change his mind the next. He doesn't promise eternal love and loyalty, then abandon us five years later when he has a change of heart. His promises are truly eternal.

Not trusting in "flesh" or in mortals doesn't refer just to *other* people. It also means that we shouldn't place our ultimate trust in ourselves! Our own strength will one day fail, as will our plans and projects. Here the book of Proverbs provides a welcome complement to the Psalms. This biblical book also teaches that "those who trust in their own wits are fools" (Prov. 28:26). "Trust in the LORD with all your heart, and do not rely on your own insight" (Prov. 3:5). Here both personal wit (including charm and intelligence!) and insight (including wisdom and experience!) do not merit our trust in the end. We will one day grow old, our minds will fail, our intelligence and charm will fade. Only God merits our abiding trust.

GOD OR RICHES?

Another "idol" that tempts our allegiance and trust is material wealth. We saw in the last chapter that riches can be an impediment for someone who wants to love God with his whole heart. We feel stronger, surer, more powerful—and sometimes even superior to others—when we have money in the bank. This is natural. Those who have a lot can rest easy, unconcerned about where their next meal is coming from. Money, perhaps more than any other one factor, can challenge our allegiance to God alone and our trust in his providence. *Who needs God when I have American Express?*

The psalmist takes up this question in several passages, noting that the ungodly man who trusts in riches will be defrauded in the end and find his hopes dashed. Good men and women will see his end, when he is uprooted from the land of the living, so they should not envy his situation. Here are his words:

> The righteous will see, and fear,
>   and will laugh at the evildoer, saying,
> "See the one who would not take refuge in God,
> but trusted in abundant riches,
>   and sought refuge in wealth!"
>
> (Psalm 52:6–7)

In the final analysis, earthly riches cannot suffice. They cannot substitute for God. The prudent investor invests in God.

The primary reason for the ultimate unreliability of riches is death. As the popular saying has it, *You can't take it with you.* This is biblical wisdom, reiterated by the psalmists. For example, the Sons of Korah write: "When we look at the wise, they die; fool and dolt perish together and leave their wealth to others" (Ps. 49:10). The wealthy have no advantage over the poor at the moment of death; both leave this world taking nothing with them. So again the psalmists admonish those who fear God to be serene. Their situation is no worse than that of the rich. "Do not be afraid when some become rich, when the wealth of their houses increases. For when they die they will carry nothing away; their wealth will not go down after them" (Ps. 49:16–17).

So what happens if Christians become wealthy? What advice does the psalmist give to those who have much? His counsel is to not divest ourselves of all we have but rather to avoid placing our trust in worldly wealth that cannot last. Thus:

If riches increase,
>   do not set your heart on them.
Once God has spoken;
>   twice have I heard this:
that power belongs to God,
>   and steadfast love belongs to you, O Lord.
For you repay to all according to their work.

(Psalm 62:10–12)

We should be more concerned with living good lives than pursuing the earthly pleasures that wealth can afford, so as to be worthy to stand before the judgment seat of God. He will judge us not on our wealth or rank, but on the quality of our lives.

These teachings are echoed by Jesus in the Gospels. For instance, he tells the parable of a rich man who pours all his attention into making his wealth increase. He has a particularly good harvest and thinks how he can expand his ability to store up all the goods he has acquired. He finally decides to tear down his grain barns to build bigger ones, and he feels very satisfied with himself, saying to his soul, "You have ample goods laid up for many years; relax, eat, drink, be merry" (Luke 12:19). But what appears to be a success in the world's eyes, Jesus sees as an utter failure. He declares that God will say to that man, "You fool! This very night your life is being demanded of you. And the things you have prepared, whose will they be?" (v. 20). And Jesus adds, "So it is with those who store up treasures for themselves but are not rich toward God" (v. 21). We must ask ourselves: To what will we give our attention? What will be most important to us? Will it be worldly wealth or becoming "rich toward God"?

My biggest crisis of trust in God came several years back when I lost my job at the factory. I work in the auto industry and the company was cutting back pretty severely. I realize that it was easy to trust in God when things were going well, especially economically. But when I felt that I could no longer support my family, the bottom fell out of my trust in God, too.

—JORDAN, AGE 53

Instead, Jesus counsels his followers to be more like the ravens and the lilies of the field (see Luke 12:22–34). Work, yes, but without worry and without setting your heart on eating, drinking, what you are to wear, or how much money you have in the bank. These worldly pursuits are for the worldly, but they are not the treasure that Christians aspire to. In the end, it is a question of priorities. One priority tops the list and gives meaning to all the rest. Therefore Jesus concludes, "Instead, strive for his kingdom, and these things will be given to you as well" (Luke 12:31). It is Christ's *kingship*—and not the worries of this world—that should concern us, enthuse us, possess us, and inspire us. This is the worthy aim of a disciple of Jesus.

A PSALM OF ABSOLUTE CONFIDENCE

My favorite psalm for reaffirming my complete trust in God has to be Psalm 91. It not only asserts the most unconditional confidence; it also goes through the deepest truths of *who* God is and *why* we trust in him in the first place.

In a way, Psalm 91 sums up all the other psalms. It places God at the center of our existence as our Creator, Defender, Protector, and, above all, Father. Sometimes we need a reminder of just how great God is, and of what he does for us. Psalm 91 is that reminder for me.

PSALM 91

You who live in the shelter of the Most High, who abide in the shadow of the Almighty, will say to the LORD, "My refuge and my fortress; my God, in whom I trust."

For he will deliver you from the snare of the fowler and from the deadly pestilence; he will cover you with his pinions, and under his wings you will find refuge; his faithfulness is a shield and buckler.

You will not fear the terror of the night, or the arrow that flies by day, or the pestilence that stalks in darkness, or the destruction that wastes at noonday.

A thousand may fall at your side, ten thousand at your right hand, but it will not come near you.

You will only look with your eyes and see the punishment of the wicked.

Because you have made the LORD your refuge, the Most High your dwelling place, no evil shall befall you, no scourge come near your tent.

For he will command his angels concerning you to guard you in all your ways. On their hands they will bear you up, so that you will not dash your foot against a stone. You will tread on the lion and the adder, the young lion and the serpent you will trample under foot.

Those who love me, I will deliver; I will protect those who know my name. When they call to me, I will answer them; I will be with them in trouble, I will rescue them and honor them. With long life I will satisfy them, and show them my salvation.

Even though I don't always live this way, praying these words reminds me of what my trust in God should be like. They inspire me, enlighten me, and calm me. I think we all need a reminder of how much God loves and cares for us unconditionally. I know I do.

Like all virtues and good dispositions, trust is never a onetime conquest. You may think you have scaled the Mount Everest of trust, finally reaching your goal, only to find a week or a month later that you have lost the trust you thought you had acquired. Every day trust must be exercised and requested anew from the Father of all good gifts. Today's trust is not the same as yesterday's, since our situations change and our relationship with the Lord matures as well. The key is to keep our eyes on the goal, knowing what God asks of us, and counting on his grace to achieve it.

NOTES

Chapter 1: The Downside of Distrust

1. "Man, tempted by the devil, let his trust in his Creator die in his heart and, abusing his freedom, disobeyed God's command. This is what man's first sin consisted of. All subsequent sin would be disobedience toward God and lack of trust in his goodness" (*The Catechism of the Catholic Church*, § 397; www.vatican.va/archive/catechism/ccc_toc.htm).

2. Rachael Bell, "The Tylenol Terrorist," in True Crime Library: http://www.trutv.com/library/crime/terrorists_spies/terrorists/tylenol_murders/index.html.

Chapter 2: What Makes It All Worthwhile

1. C. S. Lewis, *Mere Christianity* (San Francisco: HarperSanFrancisco, 2001), 62.

2. Pope John Paul II, encyclical letter *Fides et Ratio* (September 14, 1998), no. 32, http://www.vatican.va/holy_father/john_paul_ii/encyclicals/documents/hf_jp-ii_enc_15101998_fides-et-ratio_en.html.

3. Alfred Lord Tennyson, *In Memoriam* (1850), stanza 27, www.bartleby.com.

4. Samuel Johnson, Rambler essays no 79, in *Selected Essays* (New York: Penguin Classics, 2003), 169.

5. See Aristotle *Nichomachean Ethics* 2.7.

6. Thomas Merton, *Life and Holiness* (New York: Herder and Herder, 1963), 21.

7. http://justthinking.typepad.com/nordenson/2005/04/a_prayer_of_st_.html.

Chapter 3: Trust and Trustworthiness

1. Nancy N. Potter, *How Can I Be Trusted?: A Virtue Theory of Trustworthiness* (Lanham, MD: Rowman & Littlefield, 2002), 25.

Chapter 5: Is God Up to the Task?

1. Richard Dawkins, *The God Delusion* (New York: Houghton Mifflin, 2006), 31.

2. Robert Stofel, *God, How Much Longer? Learning to Trust God's Timing in Your Life* (Colorado Springs: CCM, 2005), 86.

Chapter 6: What Trust in God Looks Like

1. "The challenge contained in such tempting of God wounds the respect and trust we owe our Creator and Lord. It always harbors doubt about his love, his provi-

dence, and his power" (*The Catechism of the Catholic Church*, § 2119; www.vatican.va/archive/catechism/ccc_toc.htm).

Chapter 7: Trust as a Gift *to* God

1. Cf. among many references, Catherine of Sienna, *The Dialogue* (New York: Paulist Press, 1980), chapters 58 and 59.

2. "To understand the practical importance of the virtue of hope, let us not forget the most common and most dangerous obstacle in the way of perfection. This is discouragement arising from the faults, the temptations, the aridities, found in every spiritual life. It reduces fervor and generosity, and impedes progress to perfection. While we have confidence, any obstacle can be overcome, any sacrifice is made easy, and our struggles are crowned with victory. But when discouragement invades the soul it is without energy or support, and thus easily deterred, misguided, and confused" (Luis María Martínez, *The Sanctifier*, trans. M. Aquinas [Paterson, NJ: St. Anthony Guild Press, 1957], 59).

Chapter 9: What to Do When God Lets You Down

1. Mother Teresa, *Mother Teresa: Come Be My Light*, ed. Brian Kolodiejchuk (New York: Doubleday, 2007).

Chapter 10: Waiting for the Lord

1. Marilyn Elias, "So Much Media, So Little Attention Span," *USA Today* (March 30, 2005), http://www.usatoday.com/news/education/2005-03-30-kids-attention_x.htm.

2. Augustine, *Tractates on the First Epistle of John*, Tract. 4: PL 35, 2008–2009.

3. Jerome, *Commentary on Joel*, PL 25, 967–968.

Chapter 11: Can Sinners Trust?

1. Francis Thompson, *The Hound of Heaven*, vv. 161–70, http://www.bartleby.com/236/239.html.

2. Luis María Martínez, *Secrets of the Interior Life*, trans. H. J. Beutler (Harrison, NY: Roman Catholic Books, 1949), 49–50.

3. Cited in Bernard Nodet, *Jean-Marie Vianney*, ed. Xavier Mappus (Le Puy: Xavier Mappus, 1958), 132.

Chapter 12: What We Should *Not* Expect from God

1. Robert Stofel, *God, How Much Longer? Learning to Trust God's Timing in Your Life* (Colorado Springs: CCM, 2005), 122.

2. Quoted in Francis Arthur Jones, *Famous Hymns and Their Authors* (1902), (Kessinger Publishing, 2008), 24.

3. Quoted in Lawrence Rainey (ed.), *Modernism: An Anthology* (Oxford: Blackwell Publishing, 2007), 704.

Chapter 14: Reciprocity: God's Trust in Us

1. Robert Stofel, *God, How Much Longer? Learning to Trust God's Timing in Your Life* (Colorado Springs: CCM, 2005), 83.

Chapter 16: Regaining Lost Trust

1. See http://wilderdom.com/games/TrustActivities.html.
2. Pope Benedict XVI, encyclical letter *Spe Salvi* (2007), no. 33, http://www.vatican.va/holy_father/benedict_xvi/encyclicals/documents/hf_ben-xvi_enc_20071130_spe-salvi_en.html.
3. John of the Cross *Dichos* no. 64.
4. Pope Benedict XVI, encyclical letter *Spe Salvi* (2007), no. 43, http://www.vatican.va/holy_father/benedict_xvi/encyclicals/documents/hf_ben-xvi_enc_20071130_spe-salvi_en.html.